D1795940

R. Peter Davies

MIXED ABILITY GROUPING

Possibilities and Experiences
in the Secondary School

Temple Smith
London

First published in Great Britain 1975
by Maurice Temple Smith Ltd
37 Great Russell Street, London WC1
©R. Peter Davies
ISBN 0 8511 7075 7

Printed in Great Britain by
J.W. Arrowsmith Ltd, Bristol

Mixed Ability Grouping

In the series 'Teaching in Practice'

Running a School *by C.H. Barry and F. Tye*
Movement Education *by Marion North*
Playing-Working-Growing *by Geoffrey Ivimey*

Contents

Introduction   7

Part I Why Mixed Ability Groups?
1 Streaming: Evolution and Reaction   13

Part II Mixed Ability Classes and the Subject Teacher
2 History *Peter Davies*   41
3 English *John Vickers*   76
4 French *Tony Warnes*   97
5 Mathematics *Peter Wilcox*   116
6 Science *David Bosworth*   137

Part III The Unstreamed School
7 Preparing for De-streaming   161
8 'What about the Remedials?'   179
9 Marking, Assessing, Reporting   190
10 Conclusion   203
   Bibliography   213
   Notes on the authors   215

Introduction

Two serious questions, put by teachers in their last months of training, indicate the intentions of this book. One, addressed to a colleague discussing pastoral care with a group of College of Education students, was almost an assertion: 'Teachers don't know very much about mixed ability groups, do they?' The other, put by a university student making a preliminary school visit before his teaching practice, was an understandable reaction to his first realisation that groups at the school were not streamed by attainment or intelligence: 'Where shall I pitch my lessons — at the pace of the average or at that of the slowest?'

The incredulous answers were as unfair as they were natural. Involvement with mixed ability groups at the classroom level over a decade has inevitably dimmed, or even extinguished, the memory of initial problems, fears and suspicions. It is hard for the majority of teachers to re-think accepted, proven methods and to discount the ways of organising school and class which seem to have worked successfully. It is particularly hard when they are themselves products of the system and apparent proofs of its success.

However, it was inevitable that the attack on the selection of pupils for differing types of education at the age of eleven — and consequently for varying adult opportunities and ways of life — should be followed by a questioning of the validity of intra-school selection. The extremists had total faith in the unchanging nature of inherited intelligence and in their ability to measure it accurately. They were also convinced of the all-important rôle of that intelligence in determining performance and achievement, at the same time looking upon the many undesirable side-effects of its dominance as inevitable. It was difficult for those of us who disagreed with this view to reject it logically while we ourselves kept the selective process going in our open-access Secondary Schools.

The system of putting children into groups according to their supposed ability has been challenged on many grounds. The subjective criteria for this allocation of children to streamed or setted classes — all too frequently used — have obvious limitations. They tend, too, to act to the disadvantage of various children: the youngest members of a year group, the children from poor homes, and boys in comparison with girls. We are coming to realise, now, that groups which appear to be homogeneous may, in fact, be anything but that. We see, too, that children who have to work in a subject-based curriculum demanding many diverse skills have been graded according to a very limited set of characteristics, including a conception of fixed intelligence with which there is now much disagreement.

Researchers have regularly suggested that the amount of inter-stream transfer needed to put right mistakes in selection and grouping rarely happens. This is probably largely due to the fact that the expectations of both pupils and staff are very much conditioned by the stream in which a given child is placed. Children placed in a 'C' stream tend to accept authority's valuation of them and to behave and work according to the normative patterns of that class. Teachers reinforce this reaction by their expectations of the performance and attitude of the 'C' form based on years of experience. The pupils' attainments consequently become closer to one another. The results are threefold: many pupils fail to achieve their academic potential; the streams move further and further apart; and those groups who feel that they have been rejected by the educational system of which they are compelled to be a part until the age of sixteen suffer an inevitable social disorientation.

Mixed ability grouping has a number of aims: to give each child the lessons most suited to his or her ability; to avoid pre-judging — or misjudging — any child's potentialities; to allow each child to feel that he or she has every chance to set a personal ceiling on attainment; to avoid categorising (and often stigmatising) children who are first and foremost individuals. This surely is the logical consequence of comprehensivisation — a system which has rejected the classification of children at the age of eleven as crude and harmful.

It is, however, altogether too easy to condemn a system, not so easy to replace it. It is a relatively simple matter to pontificate about the educational, moral and social validity of de-streaming, but not so simple for practitioners within the classroom to undertake responsibility for classes of a kind they have never met before. Can the needs of the most and the least able pupils be catered for in the same classroom? What are the possible approaches, from the formal class lesson to totally individualised learning? What modifications — if any — of school curricula must accompany the introduction of unstreaming? What other changes might occur? Is mixed ability work to be reserved for the junior classes in secondary schools? Will the adoption of such an organisational pattern affect external examination results? Must accepted modes of marking, assessment and reporting be adapted? It is these types of question that this book seeks to meet: the practical problems that confront those at the 'work face' of education. Certainly the answers are not intended to be prescriptive but they are honestly offered as possibilities by practising teachers who have been involved with unstreamed children for several years.

I WHY MIXED ABILITY GROUPS?

1 Streaming: Evolution and Reaction

In the schools we went to in the 1940s, secondary school streaming seemed an integral and accepted part of the standard educational pattern — like schoolyards, outside toilets, desks with lids, canes, Reading, Writing, Arithmetic and Scripture lessons. We wanted to know how the school evaluated our progress, and this evaluation was formalised for us by the stream in which we were placed. The system was a logical one: we understood it and so did our parents. All of us saw streaming as a permanent, unchallengeable element in the pattern of education.

Yet this classification of pupils who are relatively similar in the factors that affect learning actually began quite recently. In the last decade of the nineteenth century and the early years of this one, there was a growing awareness of the differences between one pupil and another. In April 1897, Circular 395 from the Education Department (*Very Backward Children in Schools for Older Scholars*), addressed to Her Majesty's Inspectorate, suggested separate classes and special grant provisions for the least able. In the following year, *Revised Instructions* from the Department to the Inspectorate declared that 'No difficulty should be put in the way of the honest classification of scholars according to capacity and attainment.' This realisation of differences between individual pupils was accompanied by attempts to organise schools in a way that would allow for them. The Board of Education's initial revision of the 1905 *Suggestions for the Consideration of Teachers and Others Concerned in the Work of the Public Elementary Schools*, issued in 1917, stressed the problems which arose from individual variation and from a system based on rigid annual promotion. In the introduction to these revised *Suggestions* the authors recommended that 'children should be allowed to progress through the school at varying rates suited to their individual capacity'. The structure that would meet this recommendation was a classification by ability, making it possible in practice to allow groups of children of supposedly similar ability to go through school at different rates.

The impetus towards classification was increased by a vast public demand for secondary education — seen as a means to social mobility and improved status within a society that was becoming complex, diverse and democratic. Robert Morant did away with the challenge of the Higher Grade Schools by centring the system established in 1902 on the rejuvenated Grammar Schools. Twenty-five per cent of the places in the latter were to be free to pupils who had spent two years at Public Elementary Schools and who showed talents which could benefit from the award of such places. The demand for them always exceeded the supply; pressure from parents and a sense of the kudos associated with the number of Grammar School places won inevitably led Primary Schools to try to develop systems of organisation which would make the achievement of the goal easier. Some of them, for example, gave up teaching subjects such as History and Geography, which were not examinable. One Primary School was praised by the Board of Education for devising its own two-tier system of six rooms for bright pupils and four for the not-so-bright, where the latter could remain for a whole year, or longer still, if necessary. This system, the Board said, could 'render possible a better classification of scholars and . . . secure a more rapid promotion through the schools on the part of children who give special promise, thereby facilitating their transfer to Secondary and Central Schools' (the Board's 1919 Memoranda on Promotion in Elementary Schools in London).

In its early stages, streaming was obviously impossible to quantify in terms of its use on a national scale, but it did seem to meet with the approval of both administrator and teacher, and it had some support, too, from psychologists. During the eighteenth century Francis Galton had declared that individual faculties are hereditarily determined; in 1904, Charles Spearman put forward the theory that there is an inborn general ability in all intellectual processes. Alfred

Binet worked out a scale by which intellectual capacity could be measured, and by 1920 this was in use for selection purposes in Bradford. It measured inborn intelligence of a general kind, showing not only what a child *had* learned, but what he *could* learn. On this basis, some schools (the Ben Jonson School in Stepney, for example) were able to refine their streaming of pupils into the super-normal (IQ over 110), normal (IQ to 110) and sub-normal (IQ below 90).

This pattern found favour with administrators. By 1927 the Education Board's *Handbook of Suggestions for Teachers* recommended as ideal a treble-track system in which 'backward, ordinary and quick' pupils were identified, separated and taught by different and appropriate methods. Any refinements of the basic system were approved of — the Caernarvonshire system, for example, in which the top two classes of several neighbouring schools were brought together under one roof to facilitate still finer streaming. At the same time, separate curricula were worked out for the various ability groups: French, Algebra and Geometry were invariably reserved for the class designated as the most able, whilst 'B' pupils had practical Arithmetic, and 'C' classes were taught more practical subjects and given more oral work.

Many schools in the 1930s were too small to stream, but in others streaming seems to have become the standard pattern, reaching its peak during the expansion of schools during the 1940s and 1950s. There were occasional tentative criticisms: the Ministry of Education's 1945 pamphlet, *The Nation's Schools*, wondered if 'grading on this basis may in future not appear as desirable as it does now'. But instances of this kind of questioning were isolated. Butler's Education Act of 1944 ensured 'secondary education for all'; the pattern which was adopted to allow for this education of all according to 'age, aptitude and ability' was rooted in the Norwood Report's vision of three types of children slotting neatly into Grammar, Technical and Secondary School boxes. This was the synthesis of the demand for education for all and the theory that differing abilities require different educational treatments. Logically enough, children who had already been allocated to streams in the later stages of their Primary School lives, so that their accurate selection for academic or other careers would be made easier, now had to be allocated to different types of school, according to their needs, and — refining the process still further — to different streams within a particular school. This would ensure that their needs could be met together with those of their academic peers.

The system of organisation was based on 'a series of apparently common sense beliefs' (Goldberg, 1966), and clearly the logic of it was accepted by practising educationists at all levels. Daniels (1961) found that every one of the hundred and seventy-three Primary School teachers attending courses at Nottingham University at one time supported streaming by ability as an organisational base. Jackson (1964) found that ninety-six per cent of his sample of six hundred and sixty Primary Schools of England and Wales were streamed by the time that their pupils reached the age of ten. The Advisory Centre for Education, seeking to ascertain the degree to which experimentation modifying rigid streaming had taken place, in 1967 contacted over four hundred Comprehensive Schools and found in its replies — from what could well be an unrepresentative one hundred and thirty-five schools — that less than one-third were in fact experimenting in this way.

However, the minority figures do indicate an uneasiness absent in earlier years. In 1959 a Ministry publication, *Primary Education*, warned that it was the experience of some head teachers that 'in the homogeneous class of the streamed school the stimulus to learning is reduced and that the slower children appear slower still, accepting the fact that they are too often called "*only* B", and making less effort than they might' (the emphasis is mine). Similarly, at the secondary stage, the Newsom Report suggested that the concomitant of fine streaming was an increase in 'the feeling of educational inferiority and rejection in the lower forms without corresponding teaching advantages'. Some intuitive criticisms were made, too; as by a headmaster, R. G. Crow. He reported that as a departmental head in a very highly selective Direct Grant School, he was constantly aware of the continual abject failure — in examination terms — of 'D' stream pupils who, despite their lowly class status, were obviously highly intelligent. They had evidently accepted the school's judgement of them. Similarly, he saw the pattern repeated when he became headmaster of a two stream mixed Grammar School. Here 'Of fifty-five pupils who entered this streamed school in 1957 only eighteen had remained to complete their GCE Ordinary Level Course in 1962. All the "B" stream boys and all but six of the girls had left school convinced that they were "non-academic" types.'

Such arguments were, of course, countered, sometimes on the ground of examination pressures, sometimes on that of the over-large size of classes. To some, streaming was defensible for the help it gave to the less able; to others, it existed to ensure maximum progress for the most talented. The argument for the defenders of the system was impressive: it had been created to meet the ever-increasing need for precise selection and to deal with external examinations. Supported by teacher, psychologist and administrator, streaming had evolved because a static IQ could be measured, children allocated to classes, each class progress at its own pace, with minimal boredom, and any errors be put right by cross-stream transfer. Schiller's article in *The Times Educational Supplement* (1963) summarised the school's task: to 'find out what each boy and girl can do, sort them into classes accordingly, give each class the sort of work that interests them and is within their powers, and then let each class flow each year through the school like a stream'.

How much of this theorising, how many of these assumptions had been tested empirically? How much can be verified? Can we measure or predict intelligence? Is inborn intelligence all-important in academic success? Can we achieve homogeneous groups by our crude measures? Are the common factors which persuade us that a group is relatively homogeneous in one subject area equally operative in a different area of the curriculum? Are groups which we consider to be homogeneous likely to make more progress more rapidly? Ought we to select children by latent ability? Can we be sure that inter-stream transfer will enable us to deal with all mistaken pupil placements? Are there side effects of the streaming system of which we are not aware?

The challenge to streaming was developed round these questions. Were teachers using valid measures in placing pupils in their classes? Many doubted this and Jackson's 1964 survey showed clearly that in his sample of six hundred and sixty schools, the most popular means of placing children in streams on entrance to their Junior School were internal — reports from infants' schools, class teachers' recommend-ations, school tests. Indeed, some thirty-seven per cent of this sample used no objective test: a curious feature of the stream selection process if intelligence was indeed quantifiable. Was this an unconscious — or indeed conscious — attack on the validity of objective tests, supposedly culture free, as predictors of future attainment? Vernon (1957) may have voiced the fears of many when he wrote that 'One should never think of a child's IQ (or other test result) as accurate to one per cent. Rather an IQ of, say, 95, should be thought of as a kind of region or general level.' He goes on to suggest that over a period of several years — perhaps a child's Junior or Secondary School career — there is only a ten to one chance of being found between 80 and 110. The National Foundation for Educational Research considered that at least ten per cent of children were placed in inappropriate Secondary Schools, so insensitive and blunt were the supposedly objective testing instruments. This finding was a direct echo of the Crowther Report's contention in 1959 that one-fifth of eight thousand National Servicemen, studied at the age of eighteen, had been wrongly placed seven years earlier.

If the information behind the measures designed to allocate children to schools could be so inaccurate, could that same information be used to ascribe children to streams at secondary level? The Headmaster of Woodlands School, Coventry, analysed the progress of some of his first-year intake in the autumn term of 1962 (Thompson, 1965). The one hundred and twenty-nine Form One boys whose Verbal Reading Quotients (as determined in the Authority's tests) were in excess of 108 were placed in four parallel forms by alternating selection from the rank order list. These forms then followed the same syllabus and took common examin-ations in English, Mathematics, French, History, Geography and Science at the end of each of the first two terms. Sixty-two of the boys initially had VRQ scores in excess of

115 and their progress was followed — as 'selective' boys who would probably have gained a place in a Grammar School which took twenty per cent of Primary School pupils in its catchment area. Had these pupils been streamed by attainment at the end of the first term, nine non-selective boys would have been placed in Form 1A and twenty-two in Form 1B; that is, thirty-one out of sixty-seven non-selective pupils achieved better performances after three months in the school than twenty-nine of sixty-two selective boys. A similar pattern was found in the lower band of three parallel forms, and in both bands again at the conclusion of the spring term 1963.

Certainly this was not a tightly controlled experiment but it was a typical indication of the growing uncertainty of teachers about the criteria of stream selection. If objective methods were so suspect, what value did our own subjective assessment have, assessments in which we invariably, although often unconsciously, brought into operation many factors based on chance or bias? Was it any more acceptable to introduce our own 'do-it-yourself' version of the 11+ machinery which we in Comprehensive Schools had rejected so determinedly? Could children entering the totally strange world of the Secondary School be expected to respond to initial testing in a way that truly reflected their present ability or their potential?

More doubts were expressed (and confirmed) in a host of minor studies which contributed to increasing overall doubt about the traditional organisational pattern. A Primary School Headmaster in Scunthorpe, Gordon Pape (1956), found that at his school autumn-born children had three times the chance of their summer born friends of being in the top stream; at the other end of the age spectrum, the Durham Local Education Authority found that among pupils remaining in their Secondary Modern Schools in order to sit GCE Ordinary Level examinations, forty-five per cent had their birthdays between September and the end of the year, and only twenty per cent were summer born. Had these children failed to recover from the handicap of having only four terms at school before their teachers streamed them, while their older contemporaries had been at school for six terms?

Barker-Lunn's massive study (1970) of almost fifteen thousand Primary School children confirmed that in two- three- and four-stream Junior Schools, 'A' classes are older than 'C' or 'D', and, similarly, that there are more girls than might be expected to be there by chance in these top classes. Was equality of educational opportunities really being offered to pupils?

It seemed that many pupils were being placed in both schools and streams not best suited to their abilities, and also that the system appeared to work to the distinct advantage of middle-class children. Many research studies pointed to the disproportionate numbers of middle-class children found on the registers of 'A' classes. This is not the place to go into the many arguments tentatively advanced to explain this in- disputable phenomenon, but it certainly does appear that children brought up in middle-class homes subscribe readily to the ideals which the school fosters. They generally succeed right from their first days at school, where the attitudes and values of their teachers reflect those of their families. Working-class children often reject these alien ideas and expectations, being unable either to understand or to act upon them readily. The areas of language which Bernstein, Lawton, Henderson and others are exploring could well make a marked contribution to the acceleration or slowing down of progress. Research has suggested that language, far from being a mere communication instrument, controls what is learnt, the manner in which it is learnt and consequently conditions future learning. Pupils whose normal speech code is 'restricted' are seen by Bernstein to lack three things: the ability to be explicit in their use of language; the means whereby shades of meaning can be introduced by accent and subordination; and the range of vocabulary to harness language in a complex way in order to develop argument or illuminate relationships. He put forward the hypothesis that, fundamentally, the working-class child, possessing only a restricted speech code, might find communication between his teacher and himself breaking down. Whatever the validity of this thesis, certainly places in lower streams — at whatever age level — tend to be filled largely by pupils whose social status is relatively low. In streaming pupils early, have we helped lame dogs on to stiles, then pushed them backwards? Have we placed an extra handicap on those who have already had — in educational terms — a bad start?

Many people argue that although no system is perfect, flexibility will surely enable us to cope with the errors we make. After all, numbers of us will spend many hours in staff meetings, discussing the need to promote or demote certain children on the stream ladder. Conscientious, experienced teachers will be able to pick out those children who have been misplaced and correct mistakes. This is particularly so in Comprehensive Schools where merely a change of Form is necessary, not the obviously more problematic school transfer. But have we much overestimated our ability to put errors right? How many of the staff meetings we attend have participants unhappy about the decisions taken when several children have been suggested for promotion by different teachers and none has received unanimous support? There are often only vacancies for one or two in the upper stream and so a hand vote has narrowly carried this small number of candidates forward. They may later fully justify their promotion, but what about all those who narrowly miss the step up? Would they too shine in the more academic environment? Do they ever knock on the door of promotion again? Does there come a time when different curricula preclude their promotion?

Daniels (1964), using information provided by experienced teachers, found that only about one-quarter of the inter-stream transfers which teachers thought necessary were actually carried out — a discrepancy of some four hundred per cent. Why? Is it not true that in any given situation we tend to behave as we are expected to behave? Guthrie (1938) described how an unattractive, gauche, uncertain, relatively isolated female college student was transformed into a relaxed, vivacious, confident person by systematic treatment as a social favourite: frequently dated, regularly admired, always treated with respect by her male contemporaries. Animal studies similarly show a tendency for performance to be closely linked to expectation. When researchers were told that the rats in one batch were more intelligent than those in another, the 'bright' rats actually did learn maze patterns quicker than the 'dull' ones — although in fact both batches had been picked at random! Many people believe that some form of self-fulfilling prophecy could be at work in the streamed school, that children take on the characteristics of the streams in which they are placed and that teachers, as Asbell (1963) neatly put it, are too concerned with 'what to expect, so seldom with what they might effect' and communicate these expectations to their pupils.

The planarian, the rat, the chimpanzee, the dog — all have been the subjects of experimentation to support educational hypothesis, but can we really base vital educational decisions on lower animal forms? Rosenthal and Jacobsen (1968) added to the fears. Three hundred and seventy pupils in an American High School were given a test of general intelligence, a non-verbal one often used, which they somewhat grandiosely christened The Harvard Test of Inflected Acquisition. Teachers were told that this test would indicate pupils who could be expected to show an academic spurt in the near future, and twenty per cent of the children — randomly chosen — were selected. At the end of the twelve-month session these 'academic spurters' had indeed performed at a markedly higher level, raising their scores on average by some twelve points, compared with the other children's eight point increase. Indeed, the youngest of selected improvers scored on average at a six-point higher level than their peers. In a re-test situation twelve months later, when the children were all taught by different teachers (deliberately uninformed about the earlier experiment) the advantage of the 'spurters' was seen still to exist, if less markedly. Was pupil performance conditioned by teacher expectation, however communicated? Do we, as teachers, control achievement by setting ceilings for our pupils, artificial, generalised ceilings based on what we think a set of children can do?

Many researchers have since pointed out the possible operation of a self-fulfilling prophecy in English schools. The major study of Joan Barker-Lunn (1970) of four years in the lives of some 5,500 Primary School children gave marked support to this theory and so, at a much cruder level, did Whalley's interesting small study (1968) of inter-stream movement in a ten-form entry mixed Comprehensive School.

His results showed clearly that pupils who were promoted in the first term at their new school continued to improve, often to the extent of promotion through as many as three classes later. The converse was also true: those transferred to lower streams often continued along the path of demotion.

Professor Brian Simon tells a story of three hungry chimpanzees, each admitted in turn to a cage. This was littered with the boxes and hooked sticks necessary to reach the bananas hanging from the ceiling. The American chimpanzee raced round almost frenetically, before perceiving the inter-relationship of all parts of the problem's solution and gaining his reward. The Russian chimpanzee sat pondering, unhurriedly, in the corner, saw the answer and slowly, methodically, took his hard-earned bananas. The British animal — as hungry as the rest — was let into the cage, but soon sat despairingly in a corner, muttering to himself 'I'm not clever enough to solve such a problem, much as I need those bananas!' His perception of his own capabilities had been conditioned by his education, in contrast with that of his Russian and American counterparts, whose development had not been controlled by selection!

Barbara and Jean were originally placed in Form 1C in a four-form entry Comprehensive School; ultimately they gained between them six passes at Advanced Level, three of them with distinctions. How many of their peers failed to beat the system in the same way — less obviously able children perhaps, more ready to accept the school's verdict of them as they saw it in their stream placement. As Simon (1967) in his inaugural lecture at the University of Leicester pointed out: 'If you test a number of children at a particular point, range them in order, reduce that order to A, B and C groups and give each of these a different education, adjusted to the "appropriate" level what is likely to emerge?' The results we obtained convinced us that our system was operating with success — our forecasts of achievement were largely accurate. Is it not so that the pattern we had established could achieve no other result?

It has been argued, too, that, academically, streams tend to polarise, that the attainment gap between groups tends to increase markedly. This is not solely the consequence of differentiation in curricula, with some streams taking one or two languages, some doing separate sciences, others studying General Science and extra Craft. Nor is it due to the doctoring of syllabus content according to what is thought suitable for a given set of children. Teachers often talk of differences of attainment between children increasing as they progress through the school, until, ultimately, a high degree of motivation, of endeavour and improvement is evident at one end of the academic scale and a contrasting apathy and regression is apparent at the other. Many variables could be contributory factors here: Jackson (1964) wondered about parity of provision for different streams. In his study, the lowest streams very frequently were taught by the least experienced teachers who had the least remuneration in terms of salary increases for posts of special responsibility. One would think that the reverse should be true: that those who have the greatest learning problems and present teachers with more frustrations than their more able peers should surely merit more skilled teaching. It is the most difficult medical cases who are directed to our highly skilled specialists whilst general practitioners are more competent to deal with others.

Of course, not all schools approve of Heads of Departments teaching only their most able children. Similarly, not many schools would mirror the Primary School visited by Jackson (1964). Here the 'A' stream was taught in the classroom, the 'B' class met in the dining room (thus losing much of the last lesson in the morning while meals were laid out), and the 'C' Form was housed in a cold concrete hut in the playground! Many researchers have pointed to the widening gap between streams, none more pointedly than Douglas (1964). His study was of almost five hundred children born in March 1946, who remained in the same two-stream Primary Schools for the four years prior to Secondary School selection. He found a marked tendency in children of equal measured ability at the age of eight to improve their attainments if they were placed in the 'A' Form. At each level of ability 'A' stream members improved their scores, 'B' stream pupils deteriorated, most evidently in the case of the most able 'B' streamers. Douglas concluded that 'Once allocated, it seems that children tend to take on the characteristics expected of them and the forecasts of ability made at the point of streaming are to this extent self-fulfilling.'

It is interesting, too, to consider why there is clearly a greater variation in British scores when they are compared with attainments in countries where streaming is not used. Several cross-national studies have aimed at comparing achievements by pupils of like age, working in contrasting educational environments. They have highlighted this tendency for our deviation from the norm of attainment by most and least able children to be much greater when promotion through the school is on the basis of age and stream rather than grade attainment. The UNESCO Institute for Education's study of the relative performances of some ten thousand thirteen year olds in twelve countries in a battery of tests (Foshay, 1962) might perhaps be criticised in its sampling procedures but its conclusions are interesting. Consistently, through Non-verbal, Mathematics, Reading, Geography and Science tests, scores in England and Scotland reveal much larger dispersions. The study stresses that these two countries alone promote by age and by stream within age groups. The variation in curricula and in the expectations of teachers responsible for different streams lead pupils to keep moving apart in achievement standards. The other ten countries in the study use some variant of the grade placement system with initial allocation to classes being by age and movement after that being controlled by the attainment of grade academic norms. Thus, teachers try to ensure that as many as possible reach the prescribed standards for a specific grade. They try, too, to concentrate on the below average so that, though achievement scores do not necessarily cluster tightly round the mean, the extreme academic poles tend to be less in evidence.

Many teachers have remarked upon the creation of two schools under one roof which can accompany this academic polarisation — two sub-cultures which are obviously far apart in terms of social adjustment. As Sir Alec Clegg (1963) has said: 'To put a child into a "D" stream is to classify him according to his inferiority — and he knows it.' West Riding

Secondary Modern School pupils, members of 'C', 'D' or 'E' classes, were invited by him to write about what they liked and did not like about being in their class. The following are some of their comments: 'Practicly [sic] everybody treats you like a scruff'; 'People tease you'; 'Holy Joe . . . treats us like convicts'. The evident feeling of inferiority is distressing enough. There is a great deal to think about here, in fact: the questionable means by which children are selected for these classes; the undesirable side-effects when judgement of academic qualities almost becomes total judgement of the pupils as people, even though it takes no account at all of many individual qualities.

David Hargreaves (1967), studying the behaviour patterns of fourth formers in a northern Secondary Modern School found support for what so many teachers had come to accept as a fact of educational life: the higher the stream, the greater the pupils' commitment to and satisfaction with their school. Members of higher streams reflect teachers' wishes and so do not have their hair long, wear jeans or smoke, but involve themselves much more wholeheartedly in extra-curricular activities and are infrequently absent. Children in the lowest stream at 'Lumley' school all exhibit the opposite tendencies and build up a delinquent sub-culture whose interests are alien to those of the school. We have all met children whose failure (in the school's terms) is impressed on them daily and who consequently seek compensation in other values which they demonstrate in status symbols such as non-conformist dress or smoking. Their values run counter to those of more able children who capitalise on what the school has to offer. There is a latent clash here which materialises in gang formation and friction, and perhaps foreshadows the ruptures in adult society?

This social polarisation operates even in highly selective Secondary Schools. Colin Lacey (1966) traced the stages in the formation of such sub-cultures at a Grammar School, 'Hightown', whose first form intake represented only a very small proportion of children living in the catchment area. Within twelve months two distinct elements were apparent: the boys who did well and fitted in, and their peers who, after being star pupils in their Primary Schools, began to fail to meet the demands of their new school and resorted to other means of keeping their status – smoking, truancy, giving cheek to teachers, failing to do homework. 'A boy who takes refuge in such a group because his work is poor finds that the group commits him to a behaviour pattern which means that his work will stay poor and in fact often gets progressively worse.' Lacey sees this exacerbated as the children pass through the school and their relative failure is underlined.

These studies may deal with limited samples and could be criticised as atypical, but they do seem to confirm what has been felt by many teachers. If such sub-cultures exist, parallel to streaming, formed and encouraged so early and involving an uncomfortably large proportion of school children, then a reappraisal of organisational structure is called for. The nub of the problem is not the creation of a series of sub-cultures with their differing norms. It is the fact that some of these create problems which totally undermine the chances of fulfilling the schools' aims for some children and impair the chances of success with regard to others. As Freeland (1957) has suggested, 'Though segregation is said to be made on intellectual grounds alone . . . In effect it results in putting together all those more "difficult" children into a "C" stream, labelling them as inferior, and so actually creating a social problem within the school and outside.'

Streaming may be attacked on many grounds, then, for its unanticipated biases and consequences. Its very roots are open to challenge. This is not the place to enter the dispute between the relative importance of environmental and hereditary factors in the education of children and in their individual performances. Even so, the philosophy of teachers in this area must affect their approach and achievements. Pigeon (1962) concludes his study convinced that 'The teacher who stresses innate individual differences as the major factor in determining achievement, will expect – and hence tend to obtain – a wider dispersion of attainment than the teacher who believes that the environmental influence of the teaching situation plays an equal if not more important part.' The very basis of streaming lies in a capacity theory: that children whose abilities are unchanging can, as a consequence, be placed in relatively homogeneous groups. Yet many have demonstrated that intelligence scores do vary markedly over a period of time. Intelligence can 'no longer [be] regarded . . . as a fixed, unitary and hereditarily determined quality, but rather as a fluid collection of skills which are to a considerable extent developed by early experience and subsequently affected by the quality and length of the formal schooling that an individual undergoes' (Yates, 1966).

If certain factors exist that control the degree of development of intellectual powers and that cause this development to happen at different rates, so that we cannot predict the ultimate level of a given child's attainment, how can we possibly group children by perceived ability? Have we not too often been victims of our own confidence trick? Using some general criterion which we think operates in all areas of school work we have placed children in streams and expected them to achieve more or less similar standards in all aspects of their studies. We may succeed in reducing the mixture of abilities in one subject area but the limitation will not operate in another. The tendency towards achieving homogeneity will vary even from topic to topic, according to differences in the children's interest, the teachers' approaches, previous experience and a host of other factors. So it is logical to ask whether streaming does, in effect, markedly cut down a group's range of abilities. Setting across three or four broad areas of the curriculum must for similar reasons be equally suspect. Children are individuals, highly idiosyncratic and unpredictable. To allocate them to distinct groups for teaching purposes in the hope that each group will move at the same pace along a prescribed educational path is fraught with danger. It is also likely to produce stereotypes who inevitably fulfil the prophecies made about their probable development. 'The present system of public Primary and Secondary education is based upon assumptions which, even when they appear to be realistic, give that appearance because the selection mechanisms used act as self-fulfilling prophecies. But even within their own narrow terms, the mechanisms are imperfect . . .' (Glass, 1964).

The onus is on those who use streaming as the organisational lynch pin of our schools to prove their case. In recent years there has been an ever increasing trend towards mixed ability work, based on the realisation of the undesirable side effects of streaming and on the intuitive awareness that individual needs were too often given second place. The desire to create a society less divisive, less intolerant, more participatory and more democratic (but no less educated in the narrow sense) has informed the movement towards comprehensive education. This in turn has inevitably and logically brought non-streaming in its wake. Meanwhile, national and economic necessity has underlined the need to ensure that every citizen is educated to his true potential. The national pool of ability has been seen to be dwindling and for this our educational system must take much of the blame. National survival and development increasingly demands the plenteous supply of highly educated people; we cannot afford the luxury of members of society educated to less than their capacity. As Douglas has suggested, it is not the contents of the pool that are lacking: rather is it the efficiency of the pump we use to extract these contents that needs examination. At one level, for both educational and social reasons, mixed ability grouping has been embraced. The success of non-streaming is, as yet, difficult to evaluate for a number of reasons: it has only operated for a relatively short period; it has met with inevitable opposition; and it has created the need to re-think classroom approaches. But, as one headmaster (Kenneth Coram, 1962) — an early supporter of non-streaming — has maintained: 'Advantages are extraordinarily difficult to assess in any objective way — they show themselves in terms not only of intellectual development but also in terms of social development and the general ethos — atmosphere, happiness — of the class as a whole.' It is in these two areas — academic and social — that the case for mixed ability work exists.

When the headmistress of Levenshulme High School abandoned streaming she did it on academic grounds (see 'Experience with Mixed Ability Groups', *Forum*, vol. 11 no. 1). She contended that it was impossible to form and retain homogeneous groups for teaching purposes, and so she urged her staff to rethink their teaching methods in the interests of the achievements of all. Many of the opponents of mixed ability work would maintain that the converse is true — that to abandon streaming is to reduce academic standards as work rates and level will have to be readjusted to enable the slowest children to cope. It is perhaps necessary, therefore, to glance at the few detailed studies of the effects of the introduction of mixed ability work on attainment.

Goldberg, Passow and Justman (1966) saw a positive academic gain for mixed ability groups relative to groups whose pupils supposedly had narrower limits of ability. Investigating the progress of over two thousand New York eleven and twelve year olds in Reading, Arithmetic, Science, Language, Social Studies and Work Study skills over a two-year period, they studied classes of children formed by many permutations of ability groups. Using IQ scores, they first placed the pupils in five ability categories, and on the basis of this five-point scale formed eighty-six classes for teaching purposes. These varied from the narrow range (one or two ability levels, e.g. just 'A'-graded pupils or 'A' and 'B'), to medium range (three ability levels) to broad range (four or five levels). The class groups remained static for the two sessions and it was found that children placed in the broad range – whatever their ability – had the highest achievement in a large majority of subject areas. Those pupils who worked in the narrow range classes (the single ability stream) appeared never to have the greatest success.

The dangers of extrapolating results from one side of the Atlantic to the other must be recognised, of course. But in Britain, too, some work has been done. Within the narrow limits of his experiment – the study of two pairs of matched Primary Schools over a four-year period – Daniels (1961) concluded that in average IQ scores, Arithmetic, English and Reading pupils in the non-streamed schools made significantly greater gains. Others have reached similar conclusions and have stood the streamers' argument – that the progress of able children would be retarded – on its head, maintaining that 'It is in the streamed situation that this [gifted] child is going to be held back. Normally, he or she will be reduced to the pace of the slowest, for it is the essence of class teaching that the class progresses at a uniform rate' (Warwick, 1969).

Other researchers in several countries have found that there is insufficient consistent evidence to enable conclusions to be reached about the most effective form of grouping to maximise academic progress. Joan Barker-Lunn's (1970) efforts to discover the effect of seventy-two matched streamed and non-streamed Junior Schools on their pupils in English, Reading, Mechanical and Problem Arithmetic, were unavailing. She concluded that a study of average attainment gains lent no support to either organisational pattern. Her findings were not affected by a study of the teacher variable (a rare feature of research in the field): whether teachers supported the pattern adopted by the school in which they taught or not made no difference to the results; those who supported streaming but who found themselves teaching mixed ability classes appeared not to affect the overall pattern of findings.

Two major Swedish and American studies were similarly unable to offer firm guidance to educationists as to which type of class is the more likely to give all children the best chance of achievement. Reviewing the five-year progress of almost three thousand Stockholm children between the ages of eleven and sixteen, Svensson (1965) could determine no real difference in the long run, though results at the end of the first year had appeared to indicate the superiority of grouping by ability. Although 'We cannot draw any definite conclusions as to the effect and efficiency of homogeneous classes,' Svensson concludes, 'nonetheless, it appears reasonable to assume that the varying homogeneity as between the school classes we studied in Stockholm has no relation to the achievements of their pupils.' Similarly, the conclusions of Borg (1966), whose concern was with some twenty-nine thousand nine to thirteen year olds in Utah, offers no positive results. He examined progress in Science, Language, Reading and Mathematics over a four-year period in two matched, neighbouring districts and his results led him to put forward the already proven hypothesis that 'Neither ability grouping nor random grouping has a consistent general effect upon achievement at any of the grades of levels tested.'

A decision about whether to stream or not on grounds of maximising achievement cannot yet be made with any certainty. Nevertheless, the evidence so rapidly reviewed here tends to refute the traditional defence of streaming: that real progress is consequent upon the narrowing of the ability range within classes. This remains true if traditional measures like Ordinary Level success are used as criteria (Thompson, 1974).

It must also be admitted, however, that much of the argument for the wider introduction of mixed ability work is intuitive. Many have written about their personal observations of the abandoning of streaming. Many have pointed out that schools have become happier places. Whether this is the consequence of giving up a system an integral part of which is the rejection of some members of the school community, or to some other factor, it is not possible to say. I am convinced that very many more pupils see themselves as valuable and valued members of their school society. Diminished leaving rates (as reported by Caroline Wedgwood Benn [1971] and Dr David Thompson [1974]) and lower absence levels tend to endorse this view. Visitors to both the schools in which I have taught where unstreamed groups are the basic organisational unit have remarked on the children's apparent contentment, and their reaction has been amply supported by parents. Dr Thompson (1969), Headmaster at Woodlands School, Coventry, felt that 'One could say categorically that the behaviour and personal standards of all the pupils, their attitude towards work and school at the end of the two-year period was superior to what it would have been under the previous system.' Her Majesty's Inspectors, studying the first three years of the work of these children, confirmed that pupils who would normally be found in the lowest streams 'are so cooperative and amenable as to be indistinguishable from the rest in attitude or appearance . . . Not only the morale of the boys but that of the staff is higher than it previously was under a system of streaming.'

Disciplinary problems have certainly been reduced in many cases. At Settle High School — a four-form entry mixed rural Comprehensive School where I first worked with groups of mixed ability — the perennial problem of 3D, the least able form in their third year, seemed to be removed. The principle of divide and rule appeared to operate! When a large number of problem children were split up, however, the same aggregate numbers did not seem to appear elsewhere. Had their need to register protest at their obvious rejection been removed? Was this a consequence of children now having the individual attention they had formerly been denied? Certainly, through the transformation of my rôle broadly from front-stage tutor to at-elbow adviser, I found my relationships with children closer than ever, and so I was in a better position to appreciate their idiosyncratic problems and needs. Pupils too were made more aware of their different natures and difficulties. Of course, there is a danger of mockery of the least able by their cleverer classmates and of belittling which can add to the feeling of inferiority in those whose academic capacities are limited. I have seen this — but only as the exception. If we are to develop a caring, tolerant, understanding adult society, then surely the process must begin in the home and the school? Separation of pupils from one another is not the pathway to the society we want. In unstreamed groups, differing types of children can interact with one another, can readily meet those with different backgrounds and different capacities. The most and the least able will not often befriend one another, but that is not the point of the exercise. I cherish the memory of the most and least able boys in one of my Second Forms sitting quietly in a corner, Brian with John's book and vice versa. The explanation for this expressed the cooperation I hoped for: I was told that one had difficulty in making himself understood on paper so his friend was checking spelling and sentence construction whilst the other was working at illustrating the other's project study, for his powers of expression were not matched by his skill as an illustrator. Neither spoke with any condescension.

Some evidence to support these subjective impressions has been offered, though little has as yet been collected by researchers. Preoccupation has until now been with attainment — the most obvious yardstick for measuring efficiency and the most obvious and accepted of the school's duties. Psychologists, however, have paid much attention to the individual's concept of self and its effect on attitudes and performance. Adler, Maslow, Freud and others have postulated the theory that if a child sees himself as weak, bad or stupid he will seek to act accordingly and resist any attempt to convince him that he is anything different. Much literature has tied this theory to education and, debating the social effects of streaming, has suggested that the formation of low-stream sub-cultures is the invariable and inevitable accompaniment of an affront to pupils' self concepts as they fail to meet the demands of their teachers.

Borg, in the 1966 study of children between the ages of nine and thirteen, found that the introduction of mixed ability groupings brought about a marked rise in the concept of self for the pupils involved. Barker-Lunn in this country saw the same tendency, though not in classes in unstreamed schools taught by teachers who were not in agreement with mixed ability grouping. Yet this could be explained as the consequence of the teachers' concern with and attention to those children who could be expected to attain high standards in academic work. She found, too, many associated factors: less anxiety amongst pupils; greater participation of all in school activities (especially by those of middle and lowly ability); improved pupil-teacher relationships; better parental attitudes to the particular school.

In 1972 the National Foundation for Educational Research in England and Wales published *A Critical Appraisal of Comprehensive Education* and produced some interesting evidence in support of these findings, but at the Secondary School level. Although they hedged their conclusions because only twelve schools were used in the sample, the authors were able to point out that the highest participation rates in school activities amongst boys from similar schools (in terms of geographical location) was to be found in the two unstreamed schools (fifty-three per cent as opposed to thirty-nine per cent). Girls were no more involved than their counterparts elsewhere but, here again, it was pupils from mixed ability classes who were most involved in house and form teams.

Children in these schools are not only more active in outside the classroom activities but they also looked at their schools in a more favourable light than their streamed contemporaries. This was particularly true of the less able and even of the less well-behaved children. So it comes as no surprise to read that the school with the lowest percentage of children in the Fourth Forms expecting to remain at school until the age of sixteen or older (54 per cent) and until seventeen or older (24 per cent) was streamed — and also in an urban area. The opposite pole was occupied by an unstreamed rural school (with figures indicating staying-on rates of 84 per cent and 50 per cent respectively). Here was confirmation of the results of Caroline Benn who found that of schools which used one of seven main methods of grouping for First Year pupils the one which had the lowest staying-on rate (43 per cent) after the statutory school leaving age was practising rigid streaming, whilst the highest rate (63 per cent) was found in the unstreamed school.

Some evidence exists, too, for the effects of creating opportunities for children of different abilities and from contrasting social milieux to mix. Willig (1963) found that his small sample of two hundred London Junior School pupils had wider ranges of friends when they worked in groups of mixed ability. He suggested that a better social adjustment of pupils resulted from their acquaintance with children from differing socio-economic class and intelligence groups. Whilst he found little social interaction by class or intelligence between Forms in streamed schools, only the two extreme IQ groups failed to befriend each other in unstreamed classes. Likewise, Barker-Lunn found that although in all types of Junior School that she examined the majority of friendship choices were to like types, this was markedly more noticeable in streamed schools, affecting 59 per cent of friendships as opposed to 42 per cent in unstreamed schools.

Finally, I must mention an additional observation of the NFER study of twelve Comprehensive Schools quoted earlier. In 1967–8, under the Foundation's auspices, a sociometric study was made of the Fourth Form of one of the schools later to be investigated. This year group had been streamed throughout its Secondary School career and, to the researchers, one of its most marked features 'was the existence of a delinquent group of boys, notorious throughout the school for their anti-authoritarian attitude and their aggression towards younger pupils'. By 1970–71 there was no evidence of a similar delinquent group in a Fourth Form which had always been based in mixed ability units. Wide mixing was in evidence and friendship choices appeared to be rooted in Form units and the daily intercourse within them.

It would be misleading to generalise from such a limited study but, as in so many other cases, here is tangible supportive evidence of what so many practitioners have long felt. This chapter was intended to draw the many isolated strands and shreds of evidence together. Streaming, introduced because of society's demands and in answer to what appeared to be intuitive logic, brought with it little evidence to suggest that it could achieve its objectives. It failed to produce homogeneous groups across the multiplicity of activities in which the school involved its pupils — but what has also become more and more debatable is whether children at any level of ability make optimal progress, even when this is defined in narrow academic terms. Many unsought effects of streaming have been clearly seen and as comprehensivists have rejected selection at the 'macro' or school level, it has been denounced for the same reason at the 'micro', class formation stage. Selection of any sort means the rejection of some — rejection at a very early age, using very dubious measuring instruments. This has acted to the disadvantage of many who have got off to a bad start in the Education Handicap Stakes. But the handicapper has not penalised the most advanced to ensure a close finish; instead he frivolously placed the youngest, the poorest and even boys in an unfavourable position. The whole process has inevitably been a self-fulfilling prophecy which has tended to let the front runners out of the starting-gates at the head of the field, with the late starters having little chance to catch up.

The act of faith which led many teachers to turn to mixed ability grouping in the first place has received more and more support, on the evidence of both experience and a growing body of research. From this point in the book I shall assume that the case in favour of abandoning streaming is made and concentrate on the practical implications of this at the school level. Theorising is pointless, however strong the case, if we are unable to translate our theories into effective practice at classroom level. It is insufficient merely to change the structure if we cannot adapt our teaching and organisation in order to gain the maximum possibilities from the change.

Methods used formerly will not invariably be useful in the new situation; we must rethink what we are trying to do and ask ourselves honestly whether what we are doing when we are with a class, when we mark, when we report on our pupils, when we organise our schools really does marry with our objectives. The chapters that follow do not set out to declare an established model that can be used in all situations; rather they aim to describe problems which are being faced and to give some answers that seem to work in specific situations. Some methods may be transferable, some may be adapted, some may provide variations on methods already used. Certainly all the answers will be frank descriptions of actual practice in schools. They may suggest further developments or possibilities to the reader.

II MIXED ABILITY CLASSES AND THE SUBJECT TEACHER

2 History
Peter Davies

I taught Leslie and Geoff for four successive years in a hybrid of the ninth and tenth streams of a twelve-form entry Boys' Comprehensive School. It was accepted as an efficient, sympathetic establishment, concerned with the progress of all pupils equally, regardless of ability; it employed mixed ability groupings in Religious Education, Art, Craft, Physical Education, Games and Music, and set boys separately for Mathematics, Science, French and English with allied subjects, History and Geography. Yet Leslie and Geoff (and marginally, several others) appeared to have an ability in History which warranted promotion. Often advanced as candidates for an upper stream they were equally often rejected through a combination of lack of available places, disagreement of other staff or the impossibility — due to timetabling problems — of being in streams very wide apart in English and Mathematics. Could I complain? Their cases were aired regularly, discussion was unbiased, the votes of genuinely concerned staff rejected them. Yet still I was dissatisfied. Whether one attributed their work standards to flair, a good pupil-teacher relationship in this instance, the method in which we approached their work in History or their interest in the particular syllabus, their standards of achievement were high for boys labelled as markedly below average. In these days of the Certificate of Secondary Education, particularly if they were involved in one of the more appropriate Mode Three schemes being operated, these boys could have attained pass standards. Their levels of achievement in 1962 stood no chance of external recognition by their examination success and internal development within the school was stunted by their placement in a stream in which the pupils were supposed to move along together through a relatively restricted curriculum.

This was the beginning of my uncertainties about streaming. My doubts were intensified when I became Head of History in a four form entry mixed Comprehensive School in 1964. The boys and girls came from a very widely scattered catchment area — from villages and isolated farms as far away as eight miles in every direction and up to twelve in some. Their Junior School experiences consequently differed very considerably; they knew few of their peers, they were overawed by this huge establishment (less than seven hundred pupils!) and by the host of teachers. Could we stream them with confidence and accuracy? Carefully documented pupil profiles from Junior School Head Teachers clearly used different criteria (some of our 'feeder' schools had less than a dozen pupils altogether, the large ones had a top class of up to thirty-five). An initial test — whilst the children still suffered from school transfer shock — was no guide to streaming. For how long did this period of settling down last? Parental comment, personal observation and discussion with senior pupils later suggested frequently a term — sometimes less, sometimes more. Finally, our existing streams gave much to worry about — on two grounds. A school which has only four classes in every year group must inevitably face problems since each stream must — even with the most perfect of placement — cover a quarter of the ability spectrum. Mistaken placing makes the spread of ability appreciably wider and any plan to teach the pupils as a homogeneous unit is of dubious validity. Furthermore, the existing groups in the middle school appeared to contain many anomalies: children who in History lessons performed either very much better or worse than the stream norm. My colleague in the Department assured me that this had long been evident. At setting meetings to discuss the possible stream transfer of these children, there was often a vote against from a teacher in another academic area where the children showed a very different degree of mastery of the skills needed. The Leslie-Geoff syndrome had appeared once more.

Many teachers in general, and many teachers of History in particular, will have faced the same problems. Sure that some children were misplaced, that some were under-performing as a consequence, teachers — like the pupils about whom they were concerned — seemed frustrated by an apparently fixed system. Yet the obvious answer — the abandonment of streaming — takes courage. In 1965 when Michael Tucker, Headmaster of Settle High School, proposed a limited experiment in non-streaming, to which subject departments could freely subscribe, we did not seize the opportunity with whoops of joy. We were uncertain of ourselves and of the possible results. Would the most able children suffer? Could de-streaming ultimately affect external examination perform-ance — the children's futures and our public image? Would the slowest children slow down our classes? Could we give them the help they needed? Would disciplinary problems spread once low-stream, ill-motivated children appeared in every class? How would we teach them? What textbooks would we use?

These are the questions which one must honestly and inevitably think about when considering any major organ-isational upheaval. After all, looking as objectively as we could at our own previous experience, we knew that we had been relatively successful with many children in the streamed situation. Here judgement was based on obvious criteria like pupils' interest and behaviour, numbers offering to take History when choices came in Forms IV and VI, or on examination successes. The existing situation had developed sufficient interest to give us a flourishing History Society and a regularly full subscription to excursions. Why throw to one side the known and proven and take a step in the dark?

The reasons for it have been discussed fully earlier in this book but it must not be thought that we were not apprehensive. The preliminary discussions were, in retrospect, remarkably naïve. The deliberations about teaching method underlined our uncertainty: we had succeeded with class teaching, we could hold the attention of a class that way (or so we persuaded ourselves), so let us continue in this manner. The result of doing so was abject failure. Of course we modified our approach somewhat: the lead introduction to the lesson was shortened; several books were available for follow-up work; follow-up exercises were less complex than they had been with high streams. But the inadequacies were soon very obvious: how did we interest and test everyone at the beginning without talking above the heads of some or at too trite a level for others? How did we set exercises with which all could not only cope but from which they could also derive benefit by being introduced to basic information or basic concepts and to the use of them in demanding supplementary work? We wriggled on the horns of our dilemma and readjusted: short introduction, consolidation in blackboard plan or outline summary for the class to build on to ensure that the material we wanted to introduce was covered and, finally, imaginative follow-up. Now the least able coped, to varying degrees with much prompting at first, and the most able had something to go at.

But problems were still apparent — talking too much at the introductory stage, for example. One had to take up and discuss points which the class made. The consequent discussion could become protracted and six or seven pupils be bored and/or baffled. Again, the blackboard-based summary by constraints of time and space — often became over-precise and, so, constraining. Children only tried to find supporting evidence for the blackboard headings in their subsequent use of resources. They turned their backs on other areas to which their books (almost the exclusive resources at this stage) introduced them and as a result limited the breadth of their follow-up exercises. Problems of time also loomed large. Study areas were necessarily short and self-contained: 'Prehistoric Man hunts for food', for example. Methods could be summarised orally and briefly, the class could be given simple headings to follow: Animals sought; Weapons used; Dead fall method; Pit trap. An imaginary situation as a peg for the children's new-found knowledge could readily be thought of. But what happened when some were finished whilst others were still deeply involved in their work? Some water-treading exercise generally resulted: model work, more illustration, a suggested written addition to the initial study. But usually these things were seen at their true value — as merely a time consuming repetition — however the teachers might talk about adding another dimension to studies!

So, we could not be satisfied that we were on the right lines. Yet there was much that was pleasing. Behavioural problems had not arisen; the less able had not been as disproportionately demanding of time as anticipated; indeed, they appeared to be stimulated by the new situation. The most able — in quantitative terms of production and industry at least — appeared to be unaffected. Convinced, more than ever, that what we were doing was right we did what should have been done at the very beginning: we studied, above all, our aims and objectives in teaching History. What did we want children to gain from our lessons over a term, a year or their whole school life? Was the syllabus content and development the best way of trying to attain these goals? All too often aims are implicit, vague and generalised, and undefined in terms of action.

Mixed ability work certainly made us look seriously at our objectives and consciously evaluate success (or otherwise) in these terms. But having studied our goals again, we stood firmly by them; no aims were altered, no areas of the syllabus removed due to the new composition of our classes, although our priorities did become perhaps clearer in our minds. What I have summarised here is not intended to be prescriptive, but simply to be a framework for later discussion of the methods which we adopted.

As historians, we have traditionally laid emphasis on the cognitive areas of our subject. We try to satisfy our pupils' natural curiosity about the past; we want to develop an understanding of how our locality, country and world evolved; we wish to provide another dimension to the understanding of modern problems. However we put these aims into operation, teachers of History by and large accept these aims, as we did. But we also became more and more aware of other, less overt, aims. We said that we wanted children to be demonstrably interested in History, not only inside the four walls of the school's specialist rooms, but in their own environment. Skills areas were crucial: children must be guided in methods of researching answers, using a multiplicity of resources, asking further questions, expressing answers with clarity and logical development, evaluating materials or information. The levels of expertise we sought would obviously vary according to age levels, but all these goals were to be clearly before us at each stage of a child's career.

So although our aims remained the same we were more definite now about the importance we laid on our method and on skills. Syllabus content, too, remained unchanged, apart from a greater infusion of locally based history. (Here, resources proved difficult at first and directed our approach to personal observation in outside excursions and class teaching. After three years these problems became minimal, due partly to the building up of a school museum of some sixty or seventy useful exhibits by means of local begging and borrowing, but above all, to the work of three successive Sixth Form groups. They used their free time, and post-examination weeks especially to produce an illustrated sixty-page cyclostyled 'textbook' with each of its four chapters pegged to the syllabus of one year of our Department.) We continued to follow a broadly chronological approach, with a thematic or patch scheme superimposed upon it. Classes in their first year, for example, studied developments prior to 1066, the first term being taken up with prehistory, followed by the Romans, then the Saxons and Vikings in succeeding terms. The second term's work included study of the Roman army, its organisation and weaponry, defences and fortifications, Roman roads, urban and rural life. Second Formers were directed to the period between the Battles of Hastings and Bosworth, with static patches relating to such topics as the medieval town, the village, the church, the law, castle developments and the nobility being introduced. The Third-Year work ran up to the beginnings of the industrial and agrarian revolutions in Britain, took early exploration through to the eighteenth century development of the British Empire, and continued to make cross-cultural comparisons — as with Ancient Egypt in the First Year, so with the Renaissance and Reformation in the Third. Forms IV and V were concerned with the last two centuries, with emphasis in the last year on twentieth-century world history. The point to be made is that no essential modification of the content and intention of the syllabus for streamed classes was thought necessary.

When we appraised our first term's work and considered our first principles, what had we learnt that might help us to do better? Our faith was justified and our confidence increased. Losses were not readily apparent. However, I was still concerned about whether the most able could be stretched more in academic terms by better organisation of the classroom situation and about how far we were really coming to terms with the development of the skills we now set so clearly as being important.

Children would, of course, each have different levels of attainment at every stage, just as they would master the knowledge element of what we studied to varying degrees. It was logical, within the mixed ability situation and for the sake of the objectives which we now saw more clearly, to individualise work as much as possible. If children were to develop individual skills, at their own optimal pace, and each have his or her historical appetite whetted, it seemed obvious that work patterns should be individually determined within the content framework we thought appropriate. We had no experience of how to plan this, but two possibilities came readily to mind: work cards to be used by individuals and work sheets to be used by large groups or by full classes.

Ultimately we plumped for the latter on practical as well as theoretical grounds. At our stage of uncertainty we still valued the initial situation in every project, when we could be sure that everyone knew what to do. For example, one sheet which related to Domesday Book began with two extracts, one referring to the villages from which the children came. These we could read together, then the framework of the patch was discussed via the unfolding of the work sheet and questions about the work assignments were raised. I shall say more about work sheets later but from the first we ensured that any factual information we thought crucial was intro-duced early and, above all, simply in the sheet. After the teacher's introductory remarks every pupil would, we hoped, be able to get underway immediately.

We adopted the class work sheet, too, to make possible — within the normal course of work — some degree of pupil co-operation. This inevitably resulted in part from discussion of the actual set tasks at each stage, in part from discussion of the material researched for these tasks, and in part from the actual nature of the tasks sometimes set — such as a cooperative enterprise between several pupils in a wall display, newspaper, tape-recording or model. We believed, too, that if we carried individualisation too far, we could waste many of the possibilities for interaction so valuably created. Everyone coming together at the end of a work sheet — if only to look at or listen to the products of their efforts, or even to assess them as a group — was something we cherished.

Our basic hesitation about using sets of work cards in an unknown situation was that we might be wasting valuable time. Would they be a success? Might they have to be thrown away? With our spirit duplicator and with paper always available, we could, cheaply and quickly, run off materials and spend much more time on the major problem — the composition of the assignment sheets. It may seem petty to take such factors into consideration, but, nevertheless, cash and time remain the two major constraints upon our schools. A two-man History Department, responsible for six senior examination forms as well as a sizeable 'A' Level group, had many demands on its time and its increasingly expensive resources. So we now had our aims and syllabus content, and the basis of our method of operation — the work sheet. It is logical to look now at how we used these in the class situation at given points in time. The first two lessons which our 11+ newcomers received were meant to put them at ease, to give us as teachers a chance to introduce ourselves and our quirks to them and to gain at least a superficial awareness of where problems might arise. The children, on coming into the History Room, received pieces of paper directing them to nine or ten lettered exhibits scattered round, ranging from locally found fossils of ammonites to a broken tile from a nearby Roman villa, from a roe deer bone from a hyena den a mile away to a flint scraper found within a hundred yards of school, from an iron nail found in a Roman fort some twenty miles away to the printed name of a local village with its Viking origins plain in its title. The children were asked to try to arrange them in chronological sequence. The year's work was subsequently outlined round these pegs and pupils were asked to take any theme — clothes, weapons, homes, transport — study their evolution from the illustrations in R. J.

Unstead's *From Caveman to Viking* and C. W. Airne's *The Story of Prehistoric and Roman Britain in Pictures* and illustrate it themselves on a page of their exercise books with the title 'From Caveman to Viking' across their drawings or tracings.

Now the ice was broken and the children knew where they were going. The second session opened with 'What's the difference between you and an animal?' My objective here was, with the help of a blackboard time chart of some six hundred thousand years, to show how relatively short was man's existence and to pin-point some of the evolutionary stages from African apes through Java Man to our Neanderthal predecessors. The time chart was duly copied out and two- or three-word descriptions were asked for under each of the headings on the time line. Results were indicative of the children who were going to have some difficulty in work which was preponderantly based in reading and writing. I have high regard for much of the information provided by Primary School headteachers, but I find that early records can so easily become self-fulfilling prophecies; one takes the word of another teacher one respects and assumes that the character sketch often built on the very individual relationship of one adult and one child in one situation, will necessarily be a consistently valid picture. I prefer to locate problems first, then to go to records for help in defining them accurately.

Our first unit of work was 'Earliest Man in Ribblesdale' — a flexible unit in terms of time, but generally covering about five lessons and two homework sessions. In the first lesson, spent sitting on the river bank where the school stood, I involved the children in getting rid of the trappings of modern civilisation and turning back the clock to days when neither town nor road, telegraph pole nor railway, livestock nor even field walls intruded upon a landscape dominated by limestone hills, trees and river. Where would man live? Trees, pits, caves were all suggested and criticised. Evidence directed our attention to the hills. Advantages and problems were soon listed and the first introductory, short sheet gave three references (with page numbers) in the two books mentioned already, in the much more sophisticated *Britain and the*

Ancient World by J. A. Bolton and D. Richards and in
R. R. Sellman's *Survey of British History*. These simple short
tasks, to be written in rough books (with which all children
were provided by the school), went little further than our
oral lesson about homes and the animals round them.
Discussion of answers in the second lesson was linked with a
filmstrip, 'The beginnings of Man' (Visual Productions, East
Ardsley, Wakefield). The final part of the work assignment
again gave detailed, specific references and asked for rough-
book notes dealing with hunting methods, weapons, and the
uses of various parts of animal quarries. This work was
researched in the following period and homework session and
the notes were used then to write an illustrated imaginative
account of our adopted man, Ugh's, arrival and settlement in
Ribblesdale. One of the girls promptly gave Ugh a wife,
Ugheena, in the cause of female equality. Succeeding lessons
dealt with the area as he found it.

Sheet 1
Year One. **Ugh Comes to Ribblesdale**

1. Read: From Caveman to Viking, R. J. Unstead, A. &
C. Black pp.5-10
The Story of Prehistoric and Roman Britain in
Pictures C. W. Airne, Thomas Sankey & Hudson,
pp.3-9
Britain and the Ancient World, J. A. Bolton and
D. Richards, Longmans, pp.3-9, 6-8 and 27
Survey of British History, L. I. Brandon, C. P. Hill
and R. R. Sellman, Edward Arnold, pp.3-6
Settle's Past, Settle High School paper, pp.3-4.

2. In rough: Find out and note
 (i) Why did man live in Langcliffe caves? Give at least
four reasons.
 (ii) Why didn't he build pit or tree houses for himself?
(iii) List the animals he would hunt. Why were they
found here then, and not today?
(iv) Briefly describe three methods of catching these
animals.

    (v) To what uses did he put the different parts of their bodies? List them.

   (vi) What other food would he eat?

 (vii) How did he make fire?

3. *In best books:*

Using these answers and illustrating with framed, titled drawings where you wish:

  (i) Write a story 'Ugh comes to Ribblesdale', describing a family coming to this area — how and why they picked their home and how they lived.

 (ii) Draw as if from the air or make a map of this area as Ugh found it — put in everything you think important — e.g., Where were trees? Where was the river?

(iii) Do the same for the inside of the cave by drawing a plan (e.g., where was the fire? What other contents were there?)

The relatively restricted nature of the topic, the scope given to some pupils with a predilection for illustration and additional detail provided by the able pupils, who often worked faster, tended at this stage to make the time factor and the differing finishing points no problem. The exercise was rounded off with a reading or tape-recording of several extracts of the written descriptions.

The approach I used to teaching mixed ability groups is summed up broadly in this first unit, with its three parts. The introductory stage is followed by a work sheet in the form of a guided research project, in the early part prefaced by specific references and backed by relatively closed questions. The final step is the use of the researched material in a different, usually imaginary, context which ensures that information is not lifted willy-nilly from secondary sources without understanding. There are, of course, many variations at each of these stages: they can even be suggested by the pupils themselves.

Before looking at variations, however, we ought to pinpoint the problems so far thrown up: the problems of the least able (at Settle High School there was virtually no extraction from History lessons) who had to cope with the printed word and to express themselves on paper as an intrinsic part of the scheme; the problems of timing (our Departmental allocation of time was two single thirty-five minute lessons and due to the disparate time required by pupils for given project studies) the problems of resources and the much debated homework question.

The problems posed by the least able children are, of course, large. But I feel that they are often dramatised, as they are, perhaps in the question I have often been asked on courses and in lecture sessions: 'what happens when I have seven or eight non-readers in my class?', or a variation of this. It is far too easy to reply that such an unbalanced class is hardly a mixed ability group, to say that hesitant or non-readers spread through all the classes of a given year group make this a much smaller problem than what is envisaged, or to talk about the need for a remedial department to have an urgent all-out attack on literacy in the first year before placing children who, for one reason or another, have reached the stage of secondary schooling with such massive problems. All these are tenable statements. Nevertheless, there will be some pupils whose capacities are limited; what can be done for them?

School policy towards youngsters with learning handicaps or deficiencies is dealt with elsewhere (the problem of extraction totally or partially from mainstream lessons is one which has not been sufficiently aired). But when all pupils of a mixed ability unit *are* to be taught at once, what can a teacher do to ensure optimal progress? My own answer was rooted in three concerns: to ensure that all the youngsters could readily understand and deal with the introductory tasks of an assignment; to have available source materials suited to the needs of everyone; to make time available for those who have most problems.

The first concern is self explanatory. The nature of work sheets will be discussed later in this book, and I will only say now that the priorities in a given study should be introduced first in the simplest of terms, with the tasks divided into easy stages. For example, a First Year project entitled 'The

Angles, Saxons and Jutes come to Britain', ultimately
reached a level of sophistication demanding hypotheses based
on and conclusions from sketches and illustrations. It opened
in this way:

First read: *From Caveman to Viking*, R. J. Unstead, A. &
            C. Black, pp. 43-7
            A Survey of British History(Book 1), R. R. Sell-
            man, Edward Arnold, pp.35-9
            Roman Britain, R.R.Sellman, Methuen,
            pp.55-6.
            The homes of the Angles, Saxons and Jutes.
            In your best books write a paragraph telling
            1.1 From which countries these people came.
            1.2 Why did they come?
            1.3 Draw a map to show their homes before
            they came here.
            1.4 Using an atlas from the store-room if you
            need it, put on your map the names of these
            countries today.

Our class discussion and questions helped to make sure that
everyone could start work immediately and a wary eye
watched the few youngsters who might still be nonplussed.

Materials had to be provided so that the less able children
certainly had some resources available to them. At first, when
we were superimposing our new pattern on an already
streamed structure, the answer was obvious: the books
already used by the different streams generally had common
core content, though obviously treatment of topics was at
different levels of sophistication. Pupils were, of course, no
longer given their own textbook for a session; several had to
be available to them. (A hidden pay-off of the system,
incidentally, for we no longer prescribed, and consequently
circumscribed, levels of reading for our children; where their
interest was aroused, it was fascinating to see them immersed
in books more difficult than those which would normally
have been available to their class and gaining much benefit
from sections of them.) When a new topic began, two copies
of all recommended books were put on a nest of tables

occupied by three or four children (a reason for doing away
with serried rows of desks or tables) and several other copies
were always available on an open shelf to cope with
shortages. After the introductory lessons, the same books
were set out on a table by the doorway and incoming classes
selected the ones they were using on entry.

We made sure that the first questions — maps or diagrams
apart — on any sheet could be answered from the simplest
books, though the most detailed answers would clearly
demand use of several sources; as a result everyone could get
underway immediately. One unsought consequence was a
tendency for some pupils to under-extend themselves over
the books they consulted and direction was frequently called
for, especially in the early stages.

Finally, the time element — staff availability to help those
who were experiencing most problems — had to be considered. This is another factor that can be exaggerated and
the real situation distorted. Of course, the least able children
needed much help to ensure that basic work could be dealt
with; but so, too, did some children at the other end of the
academic scale who accounted for basic work easily but who
failed to use all the resource possibilities open to them, and
so did the quiet 'average' children who either under-
performed without disturbing anyone or who could easily
miss the point of a given study. All children, at one time or
another, present problems, though these may be different in
kind, and all equally merit individual attention. It nevertheless remains true that our former low-stream children
needed help more frequently than their fellows: the direc-
tions they were given were forgotten more easily and needed
greater reinforcement. So on the whole, I did spend more
time sitting with them, but it is equally true to say that it
gradually but markedly decreased.

This decrease was in part due to experience in creating
work sheets which enabled these less able children to cope. In
part too, it was the consequence of using other manpower
resources: Remedial Department staff and students from
inside and outside the school. The first of these resources
was, of course, very valuable. Two members of staff working
with one class — the one trained to deal with children with

learning difficulties, the other a subject specialist — created
an ideal situation. But it was one which required considerable
readjustment by teachers who were used to being masters in
their own classrooms, and who could very understandably
feel themselves under scrutiny, their independence challenged, their position in the eyes of their pupils undermined.
I felt uneasy at first and on show. But that was soon
overcome, particularly in view of the great advantages gained.
These came in part from discussions about the work methods
we were employing, in part from the help given to pupils —
and not merely to the least able. It was agreed from the
outset that the additional help should be available to all
pupils. Much tutorial work in lessons of the type outlined
here is, of course, advisory: helping with the interpretation of
resources, advice about methods of using materials, comment
on the approaches adopted. A considerable amount of help
could be given by a non-specialist; his brief was always to
make sure that children hitherto called 'remedial' could cope
but, when his aid was not needed by them, to give assistance
to any pupil who asked for it.

This excellent situation was, inevitably, not always practicable for the demands on Remedial teachers' time were great.
Most of my Junior classes received such help for one lesson in
every two, but some had none. Sometimes, since liaison with
the Remedial Department was much closer than it had been
previously, it was possible for pupils to continue with their
History studies in the few periods when they were extracted
from other mainstream lessons for individual help; their work
in History was used as a means to facilitate progress in
reading and writing. Students in training, when available, also
gave valuable assistance in this way. I myself was especially
grateful to volunteer helpers from Form VI for their most
helpful contribution.

Teachers' Unions have rightly been concerned with the
quality of ancillary help in the classroom. Giving teaching
functions to non-trained personnel is, of course, to create
problems. At the same time, youngsters respond well to
apparent concern with their progress as individuals, to
interest in their personal problems and to the fact that people
will give up time to help them over difficulties. I asked if

members of Form VI would be prepared to give up one or
two private study periods per week, on a voluntary basis, to
listening to children read, helping them to phrase their
thoughts and assisting First and Second Formers to understand more difficult tasks. At first this was limited to
potential teachers (later others contributed to the scheme)
and they gained much from their participation. Some, of
course, found the task a difficult one, but most were
excellent aides, well able to communicate with youngsters in
the way they did with brothers and sisters. With a wandering
brief, like that of our Remedial specialists, they nevertheless
helped to ensure that baffled youngsters were never left
waiting for attention. Nor did History classes take exception
to being helped by fellow pupils: a standard, annual,
anonymous questionnaire which they filled in for me
revealed over ninety per cent support for their presence.

Other general time pressures were experienced in teaching
History to mixed ability groups. The standard lesson unit at
Settle was one of thirty-five minutes, and the History rooms
were on the very fringe of an elongated school, built as a
series of extensions. Children, with the best intentions (and
they did not all have those) would often take some five
minutes to arrive from their previous lesson. Some would
then be painting, some modelling, some reading standard
works, others using individual source books, some tape-
recording, some writing. The distribution or collection of
materials took up more time, and so did clearing away.
Effective work time was thus very much reduced, and some
pupils were just becoming really involved when they were
told to stop.

I felt that the forty-five or sixty minute period would
provide the best solution. This proved irreconcilable with the
school's organisational pattern and so an attempt was made
to solve the problem by liaison with the Geography Department. Pairs of forms were timetabled for History and
Geography in parallel, 1 North thus having each of its single
History periods at the same time as 1 South had Geography,
the two interchanging for the subsequent lesson period. This
enabled us to take all one form's four lessons for
History, the other group taking Geography. So 1 North had

two double lessons of History per week, 1 South had a similar Geography programme. At half-term the pattern was reversed, 1 North having exclusively Geography, 1 South following a History course.

We eased some problems but only at the expense of creating others. Some children found it hard to concentrate for extended periods at first, particularly as the normal school working unit was the single period. This was a minor problem, largely solved by allowing pupils to have two parts of their topic under way concurrently if they wished — model work as well as written work for example — so that they could ring the changes. More difficult, in fact insuperable in our situation, was the problem of loss of contact with pupils for half-term periods. We had, of course, anticipated this to some extent, but hoped that it would be largely offset by the similarity of our approaches to History and Geography. Both Departments used predominantly work sheet, research-based methods so we hoped that one would complement the other and that the children would take the change in their stride. The subject change was indeed easily accepted but the adjustment by staff was not so easy. A good pupil-teacher relationship is dependent on the regular contact we were failing to provide. I became convinced that it was right to timetable the day in double lessons. Certainly it has been found in my present school that this gives the span of time and the flexibility teachers want, as well as cutting down unsettling movement time. Seeing children only once a week, however, poses problems of another kind, even if, as we feel, these are less counterproductive. At this point the History Department, with others in the Faculty of Modern Studies, is turning towards an inter-disciplinary approach which could provide the solutions we need, though a discussion of this vast topic is outside our terms of reference.

Another very different problem inevitably arose as our project became more a matter of individual work. It resulted from pupils' disparate speeds of working and progress. It was not by any means merely the consequence of the most able finishing their studies most quickly: absence, the numbers of sources consulted, time and care devoted to detail or to illustration, extra follow-up tasks suggested by pupil or teacher where interest was aroused, extra work outside lesson periods and prescribed homeworks, all contributed to pupils making different rates of progress through a work sheet. It must be emphasised that this was not a problem that regularly faced the most able, though it did confront them on occasions when interest led to their producing much extra work outside the lesson framework. The essence of work sheet tasks, once basic information has been found from relatively closed questions, is that they should move to a more open-ended situation in which pupils of all abilities can be stretched. The detail and depth of study attained by some pupils will, consequently, be as time consuming as the slow reading and writing of others.

It is a common fallacy that the most able children are not academically stretched once homogeneous grouping is abandoned. It is rather the reverse that is true, for, instead of teaching to the middle of an 'A' stream, teachers now try to ensure that every member of a class is extended. The essence of individualised work is to create opportunities that enable the brightest children to pursue themes in depth by using a range of resource materials, at an appropriate level rather than a standard textbook. Indeed, I have often suspected that it is the middle band who can suffer unless we are alert to the problem in a mixed ability context. We concern ourselves with the least able because of their obvious problems: we look closely at the work of the most able because of apprehension lest they are not fully committed to work, because of the pleasure we derive from their efforts or even because of self-congratulation; but it so easy to overlook the quiet, undemanding, underperforming 'average' child. However, though the different finishing points were not necessarily related to ability, they were sometimes a problem to be dealt with.

There were several answers to it. One, of course, lay in the nature of the assignment sheet. In a Second-year study of Medieval Village Life, for example, the first three tasks dealt with essential material: a physical study of the village of the people who made up its population and of their agricultural work patterns. The remainder, to be dealt with in any sequence by pupils, provided pegs for the study of homes, dress, entertainment, food or law and order, topics which were regarded as more peripheral in importance and idiosyncratic in appeal. Thus, when all pupils had completed the opening three sections, it was possible to call a halt at virtually any stage, by announcing to pupils that the topic would be completed one or two lessons hence and that the section being dealt with should be completed by that time. Areas not covered by some pupils could be sketched in for them by reading out the work of others, or they could study appropriate models, films or strips.

Two other obvious solutions were to have in readiness either the next work sheet or a follow-up study task. Work sheets were always meant to be self-explanatory — necessarily so, since children were to work through them independently and since some might be absent from the introductory stage. Pupils could therefore launch into them with the minimum of oral guidance. In many cases, too, it was possible to get children to pursue their interests in supplementary studies. A boy completing a study of everyday life in Tudor times could thus be asked to go on to look at travel by sea as being complementary to the work on inland transport which had been his first task. Study of one part of the topic in greater depth, a local study or a cross-national comparison were often suggested too. For example, a study following an assignment based on homes in Britain in the period before the Roman invasion directed pupils to tasks, with accompanying references, concerned with housing in Egypt in early times, life in a local hill fort on Ingleborough, or the intricacies of making a wattle and daub hut (elaborately described in Hans-Ole Hansen's book, *I built a Stone Age House*).

This raises the problem of resources: not only books, for much follow-up work, as well as initial assignments, could involve two- or three-dimensional work. Cash was, as always, a restraining factor. At first we had only the basic textbooks formerly used, supplemented by long loans from the school library. Thereafter, annual requisitions ensured that supplies of basic texts suitable to the varying needs of the children were maintained; they were much more diverse than former orders. Useful core books, referred to on work sheets, were often ordered in small quantities of a dozen or fifteen, and we also recognised that different forms of presentation appeal to different children. Many detailed works — dealing with specific subjects — homes, clothes, medicine, transport, arms and armour, castles, sport or the theatre, for example — were ordered in pairs or threes for our Departmental reference shelves, so that our regular plea after listing reference books at the opening of assignments — that pupils should also consult any suitable school or county library book — could become more meaningful. Much money, however, had to be directed away from books in order for us to keep the goodwill of fellow Departmental Heads, who were often generous in times of need. It was thus used to provide readily available supplies of paint, brushes, card, blank paper, scissors, glue, strip viewers and tapes so that children could choose how they would approach their tasks.

Books posed problems of another sort, to do with homework. If a school believes in the values of homework: that it enables children to pursue their studies in greater depth than lesson time allows, and that it directly or indirectly involves parents and encourages independent work, then the release of books to be taken out of school and the consequent losses that could mount up must be considered. When everyone had one book allocated for the year, checks and the providing of replacements were simple matters. Now that one child could consult several books in a week, how could we keep track of loans, when teaching time was very limited? The problem — seemingly small — was not easy to solve in anything but an imperfect fashion, involving much record-keeping caused by children's absences or the need of some pupils for several source books to do extra homework. Our method was to tell every pupil to take one source book to help with a homework session; then everyone should return one book in the following lesson. Extra books borrowed were then listed before children left a lesson. This plan was, I must confess, often thwarted, when books had to be collected by monitors during registration periods so that they would be available for other classes. Other solutions were less satisfactory: for example, signing books in or out at every lesson proved very time-consuming in our short lessons.

Another idea that misfired was in injudicious decision to restrict homework to follow-up work from rough book notes made from source books during class time; that soon proved as impracticable as it was hampering in terms of progress.

These, then, were the problems we met — or the problems of which we were aware! A lesser challenge, as in any mode of teaching, was to provide a variation of approach to work. At first we had blithely seen the work sheet as the answer to all the questions thrown up in the teaching of History to mixed ability groups and, indeed, it ultimately served as the basis for perhaps eighty-five per cent of our work. But this could be stultifying and neglectful of the opportunities offered by classes containing children with a host of different interests and capabilities who consequently produced a great diversity of response to any given stimulus. The class lesson consequently still had its place, not merely as an introduction to a work sheet. For example, using a series of wall diagrams, I found it very worth while to study the Battle of Bosworth with Third Year Forms. In another lesson I covered the blackboard with sheets of card to make it represent a longitudinal section of the tomb of the Pharaoh Seti I; we removed the cards as we opened each hidden doorway, to take First Formers into the Valley of Kings, as a grave robber might have done. Other class lessons evolved round listening to a story — Drake's 'singeing of the King of Spain's beard' for example — or to a tape-recording of an inverview with Anne Boleyn, shortly after her marriage to Henry VIII (my wife's Welsh accent always caused historical distortion!). This method proved acceptable if the topic was short, self-contained and exciting. Discussion in groups in the class was stimulated, answers reported back, opinions exchanged and the set follow-up work was as open-ended as possible. It looked for imaginative perception of situations, not merely recall of the class lesson; as for example, the children imagined the work involved in building Seti's tomb, the methods employed and how secrecy was maintained, or the use of such burial methods in preference to pyramids. I can accept David Bosworth's reservations about the class lesson in a linear subject area like Science, but I would still contend that the variety of reactions to given themes or topics, the realisation of wide ranges of possibilities, the consequent opening of avenues of enquiry, and the appraisal of ideas by peers, provided a most valuable and acceptable approach to a topic in History.

Variation was also achieved at each of the three stages of the development of a theme — the introduction, the guided discovery stage and in the follow-up which used researched material in a new context. The introduction of any subject is, of course, wholly idiosyncratic and my efforts to stimulate interest in this lead lesson were very diverse. Occasionally I used a filmstrip (Common Ground and V P produced many which I found useful) or slides (our own on-site photography, sliced up filmstrips encased in slides where a strip was not found to be totally suitable, or purchased sets, such as the many excellent ones of castles produced by the Ministry of Public Building and Works). Sometimes I would read a story or poem; at others, play a specially made-up tape, or else put on a display of models made by children in previous years, as of homes before the Romans, Roman military machines, or the medieval village. As a back-up to any of these approaches — or even as an introduction in itself — I gave classes a short questionnaire to be answered on a visit to a site — Fountains Abbey or Hadrian's Wall, for example.

The ringing of changes in directing research or discovery was not so easy. The most usual approach was to ask the class as individuals to find out the answers to specific questions before proceeding to use the information they had gathered in a series of exercises, as in the following sheet:

Sheet II

Third Form   Elizabeth defeats the foreigner
                Why did Spain declare War on England?

The Work of the 'Sea Dogs'

References:
JOHN HAWKINS
Kingsway Histories (Book III)
E. Wynn Williams, pp. 69-72

A Portrait of Britain under the Tudors and Stuarts
M.R. Price and C. Mather, pp. 77-8
Britain under the Tudors and Stuarts
D. Richards, pp. 117-18
The Tudors and Stuarts
R.J. Unstead, p. 21

DRAKE
(a) 1572 voyage: *A Portrait of Britain under the Tudors and Stuarts* p.78
    Britain under the Tudors and Stuarts p. 118(b)
(b) 1577—80 voyage: *Kingsway Histories* (Book III) pp.63—5
    A Portrait of Britain. . . . pp.78-81
    Britain under the Tudors and Stuarts pp. 118-20, 158-9
    The Tudors and Stuarts pp. 21-2

ELIZABETHAN SHIPS
    The Tudors and Stuarts pp. 25-8
    The Elizabeth Ship G. Robson (*Then and There Series*) pp. 5-12, 17
    A Portrait of Britain p. 80

Research (in rough books)
  1 Where did Hawkins sail to make his profits?
  2 Why did he choose this area?
  3 What happened on the voyage of 1567 after he had sold his cargo?
  4 What was the importance of this voyage?
  5 Where did Drake attack the Spaniards in 1572?
  6 What was he aiming to do?
  7 How did he carry out the attack?
  8 What were a) The real reasons?
             b) The official reasons?
    for Drake's voyage of 1577-80?
  9 Describe the route he took.
 10 Who was Doughty? What happened to him?
 11 What successes did Drake have in the Pacific?
 12 Where was New Albion?
 13 What happened to Drake when he returned to England?
 14 Describe the ship on which he sailed.

15 Jot down notes of the points you are likely to make in a
    playlet performed in class if asked to play the part of King
    Philip of Spain when told of Drake's work in 1578.

Follow-up work (in best books)
1   Draw a map or diagram to describe the slave trade.
2   Write an imaginary conversation between Hawkins and
    Raleigh telling of the events of 1567.
3   Write extracts from the imaginary log book of Drake,
    describing the voyage of 1577-80, mentioning events of
    1572, his reasons for this voyage, what happened, and
    give information about the **'Golden Hind'**.
4   On the blank map of the world provided, insert Drake's
    journey.
5   Draw EITHER a plan OR a sketch of his ship. What do
    you think were the most uncomfortable things a sailor
    with Drake would have had to put up with?

This work sheet is set in the context of a series of studies of
Tudor control of the nobility and church and their attempts
to resist foreign influence in the country. Other contributory
factors to the launching of the Armada were dealt with in a
subsequent class lesson based on developing a sketch to add
other factors, like English help to Dutch rebels, the execution
of Mary Queen of Scots, and Elizabeth's religious settlement,
to 'the work of the sea dogs'. Sometimes children were asked
to work in groups on their assignments. Many teachers,
having children working in this way would perhaps give each
member of the group different areas to research. Five
assignment sheets for a class divided into five groups would
result in one member of each studying perhaps the motte and
bailey castle, one the shell keep, another the rectangular
keep, yet another the concentric castles, and the last member
might look at the diversity of methods employed when
attacking such fortifications. I tended not to use this
approach very frequently because partial pictures tended to
result, with many pupils gaining only a glimpse of the areas
studied by their colleagues when these were reported back. I
preferred to allow all the children to attempt all the basic
discovery work, then to do varying tasks in follow-up,

consolidatory exercises, so that they would all have a clear overall picture of the evolution of the castle, for instance, but each would have a more detailed, developed knowledge of the area which particularly interested him.

Choice is an important element in creating a favourable learning situation. Where possible, if I thought that my objectives could be attained in several ways, I would offer alternatives. When they were studying Roman Britain and trying to realise the sophistication introduced by the invaders vis-à-vis the life styles of earlier inhabitants, First Formers were invited to go in any order through a series of areas of study, ranging from town to country life, Hadrian's Wall to the army to Roman roads. A few covered all these topics in a seven-week period, most covered three. Some also worked out additional study areas and tasks of their own — dress or entertainment, for example — which I approved and for which I then suggested sources. Similarly, in the supplementary work devoted to medieval village life mentioned above, pupils pursued the themes of homes, dress, entertainment, food or law and order in any sequence they wished. Often they would not cover them all, but would savour some elements of the life patterns of people they had studied in their earlier researches.

Teachers will, of course, be able to suggest a multiplicity of tasks according to materials available to them. Limited use can be made of documents or preferably, as I found, their transcripts; some tasks can involve making observations or conclusions from models; others can ask for researched material to be expressed in diagrammatic form (information about man placements at Hastings, for example) or using graphical media (maps of the discoveries), although these methods are more often useful for consolidation studies. Where possible we made use of the locality and children went out to sketch or record observations from local sixteenth- or seventeenth-century houses, from the church or from nearby field systems. They responded well on the whole to the trust and responsibility given to them, particularly as it was generally only a few at a time who were out of school and as privileges granted can also be withdrawn!

The element of choice of study also presented the

opportunity for some team teaching. I would not for a
moment fasten this form of practice to mixed ability work,
but, within the bounds of the subject discipline, it did give
our Department a chance to function as an entity rather than
as individuals. Certainly it was an opportunity for cooperation based on shared experiences, for us to pool ideas
on approaches, to learn from one another, to capitalise on
the special expertise our colleagues might have. It also
allowed children choice of topics to study, of friends with
whom to work, even of teachers to act as their guides. These
advantages can, of course, be offset by the constraints which
may be placed on individual teachers in terms of subject
approach or content, whilst the whole operation can be
nullified by teachers who are totally out of sympathy with
each other. I do not wish to use this sketch of possible
approaches to mixed ability work as a vehicle for pressing the
virtues of team teaching; I simply mention that the possibility exists, and that it is perhaps easiest to use when
unstreamed grouping is adopted, as the following example
may demonstrate.

When studying Roman Britain with the First Form my
colleague and I devised a simple joint approach. He, an ardent
Romanist, delivered the lead lesson, based on a collection of
slides showing remains and reconstructions from many parts
of the Roman Empire, to the two classes which were
following parallel timetables in history. This was followed
by a similar description of remains in Britain, supported by
model reconstructions made by children in previous years.
The sixty-five children were then invited to pursue one topic
from a list comprising the Roman town, villa, roads, army, or
Hadrian's Wall. I was to be responsible for the first two of
these topics in my normal teaching room, where the
appropriate books, models, slides, strips and visual aids were
housed, whilst my colleague retained all the materials
necessary for the projected plans of work on the other
subjects. Although we did have to ask a few children to
postpone their choice of an individual topic when one room
became overcrowded, the system generally operated successfully and both pupils and staff were able to be involved in
work in which they were especially interested, with obvious

benefits.

Variation at the final, consolidation stage was eminently possible. The only essential criterion of its suitability was that work should not be merely repeated from sources but should be gathered, organised, discussed and presented in a manner differing from that used by any of the books consulted. The most obvious method of doing this, and of consequently ensuring that dimly understood material was not copied verbatim from a text to a pupil's exercise book or sheet, was to create imaginary situations. This was another determined attempt to move from the relatively closed, information-seeking tasks to the open-ended project which used the acquired material. The able children who had often found out more — both qualitatively and quantitatively — about their topics were now pressed to introduce, order, explain, develop and even go beyond their findings, and everyone was encouraged to try to probe the reality of a situation which would entail further researches instead of a mere cold report. Eye-witness accounts, interviews, diaries or log books, letters, reported discussions, plays, guided tours, first person accounts, even menus, all found their places on work sheets as I have shown elsewhere (Davies, 1970). Children were usually invited to illustrate when they found it appropriate or if they so wished. Occasionally, however, it seemed possible and valuable to formulate tasks which were dealt with in graphical terms. These could take the form of a labelled or illustrated map (to depict events in Magellan's circumnavigation of the world, for example) or a *Dandy*-style comic strip, with caption notes describing the stages involved in making a long barrow, for instance. A Civil War sheet opened with the instruction to read several sources relating to participants in the struggle. Then the class was told to trace or draw a Cavalier and a Roundhead on facing pages and, using red for the former and orange for the latter, to shade in blocks provided on the sheets — mere block typing of titles such as The Navy, Roman Catholics, Scots, Merchants. These were then cut out by the children and glued on to the relevant sheets where their illustrations were drawn. Usually, because my own inadequacies counselled sympathy for the non-artistic or the ham-fingered, illustrative work, like modelling, was set as an alternative only!

Much consolidatory work was planned, too, for groups of children, rather than individuals — not merely to create a different approach to work, but also a structure which demanded the cooperation between pupils which I always tried to foster. Situations that required joint planning, discussion about content and its use, expression of view-points, evaluation of their relative merits and use of a range of skills which might not be at the command of one individual, were all seen as an intrinsic part of our courses, contributing positively to the objectives we had set ourselves. Sometimes, then, the class was directed to work in groups. What methods of group formation were to be adopted?

Groups could, of course, be formed on the basis of many criteria: sex, interest, ability, possession of diverse skills or friendship. In practice all except ability were used. To replace streaming at the macro level by grouping based on similar measures at the micro, intra-class level seemed to be a nonsense; for the dangers of labelling, of misplacement, of individual acceptance of group norms would all continue to operate. Groups were thus generally self-selecting, on the basis of friendship or interest. At first my feeling was that these could well become ability groups and reserve pro-cedures were held in readiness, whereby I could ask each child to pick two friends with whom to work and then combine pairs of these threesomes. This plan was never adopted mostly because the need never arose, and partly because I suspected that counter-productive divisions might result from imposed groupings. Another possible method of forming groups was by linking children who possessed, corporately, a range of organising, literary, artistic and practical skills. This scheme was occasionally operated, but it never seemed to function as well as when children selected their own groups. Strangely enough — or so it seemed to me at first — groups which were not too small (having at least four members, and usually more) could rarely have ability labels put on them. Subjective observations tended to support later research findings that even if most and least able did not often befriend each other — though they often chose the same interest topics — all other permutations of apparent ability were likely to occur. In retrospect, I feel that even had what were apparent ability groupings formed naturally, it would have been wrong to disturb them. The pupils themselves had chosen them and I made sure that all were given equal attention and facilities to undertake what they wanted to do, so no hidden meaning could be read into the structures by the class. Anyway, as a group approach to work was invariably followed by a more individualised assignment and as youngsters' alignments often tended to be short lived, more damage could be done by my intervention and (whatever I might say) by the many intentions inevitably, though falsely, imputed to this.

Group situations tended to be of two types. One was the compulsory study group, typified by a Second Form topic dealing with castles. Section 1 of the study was directed towards finding out about the nature and purpose of the various structural elements of motte and bailey castles and to reinforcing and demonstrating understanding of their functions in an imaginative piece of work, based either on a Saxon labour force building such a fortification or on their later attack on the product of their work. The evolution of the castle was then traced via a series of relatively fixed-response questions bringing out the differences between motte and bailey and shell keep, why the motte was no longer used and the rectangular keep developed, methods of siege warfare and the accompanying dangers to besiegers as well as besieged, later sophistication in overall castle structure — the gatehouse, the barbican, the concentric pattern, and the development of gunpowder which was to change the whole conception of the castle. Ultimately, the class was instructed to:

1 Split into groups of five or six to prepare wall displays entitled 'Castles of the Middle Ages'.
2 Suggested tasks (but you may add or leave out any you wish):
   Guided tours of castles.
   Sketches of important features of castles.
   Stories, poems, diaries or plays about sieges.
   Interviews with castle builders.

Diagrams to show the strengths and weaknesses of castles.
Illustrated time lines to show developments.
Models of castles, castle sections or siege weapons.
Paintings of siege scenes.

(Write or draw on only one side of your paper so that displays may be mounted.)

3 Appoint a group spokesman who will
(a) Make a list of what everyone is going to do when you are at the planning stage.
(b) Answer any questions from the remainder of the class when they are marking and discussing your completed display.

Here, each member could follow up his or her own choice of topic while still having a clear mental picture of the overall pattern of development. Each pupil had to describe his or her work load, and often written *and* illustrative work was requested from individuals thought to be malingering. This ensured that one or two well-motivated group members were not carrying their fellows. The values of cooperative involvement, especially the need to reach group decisions, were evident in this work and much that was useful resulted from the formal criticisms each group was asked to make of the others and of themselves, especially in terms of the criteria for assessment to be adopted.

Similarly, group enterprises could be offered as alternatives to individual work, the two happening concurrently. As a culmination to a series of different tasks relating to the outbreak of the Civil War in England, the composition of the two opposing forces and their initial advantages, and finally to the course of events between 1642 and 1646, Third Formers were given choices involving imaginary diaries from troopers in one of the two armies, news-sheet extracts from the period, or were directed to

Consult E. Heeley's article on Marston Moor in *The Dalesman* and A. Woolrych's *Battles of the English Civil War*

Then, in a group of three, four or five, work to produce a tape-recorded production of Spectorama, a television programme which might have appeared on 10 July 1644, discussing the war's progress up to that date, with particular concentration on the course and consequences of the Battle of Marston Moor.

All the examples of work so far cited have been found in the syllabuses of classes working in the first three years of an all-through Comprehensive School. Does this necessarily imply that mixed ability work in History is only practicable for three years? This is not necessarily so, but it is a probability, given the present nature of the examination structure. Examinations at 16+ have weight and sophistication of content and, above all, methods of assessment which, until recently, were based on a somewhat blurred definition of the skills to be assessed. They have a marked backlash effect on teaching methods in schools. While the emphasis in G C E 'O' Level examinations is on content and assessment via essay questions, which often confuse examinees as to their intentions, problems will arise. The advent of the C S E has given teachers the opportunity to become more directly involved in the examination process, to emphasise areas and skills they consider important, in the proportions they see desirable and in the manner they consider appropriate. Many have wished to examine candidates' work over the whole of a two-year course, where they might have source materials available, giving a less prominent part to memorised facts and a more significant rôle to the comprehension, perception and analysis of history. They would prefer to look for skills involved in the development of extended studies in depth, and to see shorter exercises involving the application of facts discovered in different contexts and in the study of content which is in part localised. The C S E Mode Three opportunities have introduced these elements into assessment methods. Several G C E examining boards have also re-appraised their work honestly, made their objectives specific (the Joint Matriculation Board has done this), have begun to examine these objectives formally (the University of London has a planned introduction of multiple-choice questions for this purpose) and have set out to lead students by revealing a hitherto hidden structure in their essay questions. Nevertheless, a number of chance elements still make the single examinations an uncertain one; the skill of teachers; the 'spotting' of topics (and even of questions); candidates' fortunate or unfortunate choices for revision; their performance on a good or bad day; the degree of mastery of unsolicited skills such as speed of thought and writing or the ability to develop an argument pithily in a limited time. In addition content areas must be applicable to very many students if the examination is to be practicable and feasible from the Board's point of view. Hence there is still a wide division between schools preparing candidates for traditional examinations and those in which History teachers have embraced Mode Three possibilities at C S E and employed course and project work in their assessment mechanisms. The division still exists, too, even if it is often less marked, in schools where Modes One or Two have been adopted.

While very different methods of assessment are used, courses will inevitably differ too. Thus mixed ability grouping becomes difficult if not impossible without either persuading a G C E Board to accept a Mode Three scheme or opting out of one of the two major public examinations. The Associated Examining Board have many times demonstrated their willingness to listen to such questions with an open mind, the Joint Matriculation Board is at present carrying out experiments involving school-based assessment. How many of us, bemoaning the problems we face due to the constraints of Ordinary Level, have really tried to use every channel offered by the system? Some schools have already opted out of Ordinary Level and placed all their eggs in the C S E basket, so creating mixed ability groups in the fourth and fifth years of secondary schooling. Their intentions are admirable, their courage laudable but one wonders about the effects of their faith on pupils' careers. Many institutions of Further Education and many enlightened employers will stand squarely behind their vision, but how large and influential are these numbers? The experienced and aware amongst educationists know full well that many passes at Grade 1 in C S E will equate with like grades at 'O' level, but for many its parity is with the lowest grade of pass in the latter examination.

It is my experience, however, that mixed ability groups can be taught in the upper secondary years. A system enabling students to make virtually individual choice of course by timetabling several 'O' Level, C S E Level and Internal Certificate Level courses at the same time and allowing free but guided student choice can, even under present conditions, result in mixed ability groups in History in the fourth and fifth years. I certainly found this to be so for a multiplicity of reasons after the course had run for a year or two and able children selected the C S E course . . . because of the local history in it', ! . . .'because I only need G C E English and Mathematics', ' . . . because I'm scared stiff of exams', or, openly, ' . . . because I've heard that "O" Level's a cram course and I wouldn't enjoy that'! Perhaps Vicky's message had got through. Here was an intelligent girl, now a teacher of History, who had been a member of one of her school's first mixed ability groups and for whom 'History in the lower forms and in Form VI was super, but not that "O" Level course!' Whatever the reasons, in that school, where there was an absence of even any internal examination work, and all pupils followed C S E or 'O' Level courses, my C S E groups regularly contained very able children and some whose capacities were very limited.

With these groups I unashamedly and overtly made plain my conviction that the methods embraced in the lower years of the school taxed all pupils, regardless of ability. Thus the methods outlined in this chapter were repeated totally in the upper school, as for example, in a work sheet on Roads, 1760—1970. Here a series of references, together with tasks and observations to be undertaken locally, guided students' writings, drawings, maps and conjectures about local and national roads at different points in time. Throughout the study of modern Britain and the twentieth-century world, the work sheet was an integral part, indeed the key part, in our approach. Our objectives had not had to be modified due to outside agencies, and achievements were, relatively speaking, still linked with enjoyment. It is interesting, too, to note that pupils entering from this on an Advanced G C E course in History were able to cope — in large part, I feel, because of the work study methods they had mastered in this foundation course.

Inspired — or pushed — by Vicky's verdict, which confirmed what had been obvious to me for some time, I ultimately made more and more use of these means in preparing candidates for 'O' Level. Hitherto, I had been blinded by the need for all candidates to proceed through a course, very heavy in content, at the same maximum pace. All had to cover the ground, all had to master the skill of essay writing and to churn out answers in a restrictive thirty minutes after committing masses of facts to memory. Classes in excess of thirty in a four-form entry school (where many of the most able boys had opted to study a science by the time History made its appearance on the timetable) also posed problems in an examination course supposedly designed for the uppermost twenty per cent of the national school population. Chalk, talk, tests, essays and nervous exhaustion (of teacher and taught!) had tended to be the hallmarks of my course. Work sheet methods, introduced late, enabled pupils to cover the ground, each at their own pace, some spending many hours each week grinding away outside the classroom. But the work sheets did little to meet other demands: for following up themes which tapped interest, concentrating on skills not assessed in Ordinary Level work, dwelling on local developments of national issues, looking at history on the ground, among a host of other needs. Hasten the day of the common examination for students of 16+ as long as the methods employed allow developments on Mode Three lines! Mixed ability groups and the fostering of natural, individual potential to its limit, will then be practicable and selection will be totally abandoned. This will do away with our pathetic postponement of decisions such as the decision to adopt common core syllabi (in terms of content) for G C E and C S E candidates in the first year of their examination courses so that transfers can be made after the point of first selection at 13+.

Teaching History to unstreamed groups can work, if it is

rooted in two foundations: hard work and a preparedness to see pupils as individuals. Preparation demands a certain expenditure of energy but, in the classroom, the situation is indubitably one in which the teacher is placed under enormous pressure. Constant readjustment is called for to deal with children of diverse abilities and different problems have to be tackled in different ways at the same time. My own subjective conclusion was that there was a marked benefit to pupils and teacher (if I can still use that term — adviser, even fellow learner, might be more appropriate). Here was a way of getting much closer to the achievement of the aims I set myself in teaching History; pupils gained accordingly — and their Ordinary Level results didn't even deteriorate!

3 English
John Vickers

'What am I thinking about? I don't know. My thoughts are
all muddled up, not knowing whether to stop on at school
or whether to leave. What can I do if I leave? I just don't
know. The people around seem to know just what they're
doing, some leaving, some staying, but I'm in the middle,
just not knowing.

'What a life if you're all fed up, every night, hardly
anywhere to go except if you save, then what do you save
for? To blow it all in one night. What a dead place it is
round here. I just feel like walking on a sandy beach late at
night with one special girl under my arm, and just being
away from here. Free, free as a bird.'

Ian is offering me a starting-point if I am capable of taking it
up. When he passes it to me to read, I need the time to talk
with him, confidence that he will listen, some notion of
where he might go next. All this to come from what we know
of each other, and an atmosphere of on-going work in the
classroom which will allow me to move naturally from one
person to another, and to talk with individuals and groups.
He is one member of a class of about twenty-eight people
who need to be led to a stage where this sort of working
relationship is possible.

I don't think there are any easy or quick ways of bringing
this about. Nor is there any one way of shaping English
lessons so that different individuals can grow through them.
Much depends on the sensitivity of the teacher, on his knack
for spotting the signs in a youngster, his intuition for the
right moment, his knowledge of appropriate material, his
understanding of the people he is working with, his willingness to do what he sees is necessary. If we are to work from
the assumptions that a mixed ability group reflects the

conviction that each person is to be valued for himself and that work in English involves starting from where the young person is and leading him on from there through reading, writing, talking, then it seems to me that these are some of the demands we need to make of ourselves in doing our job. As I see it, the job involves befriending the youngsters in one's care, supporting them, earning their confidence, discovering what help they need to express themselves, sharing some of the magic that has caused men to write, and in this way taking them into some of the depths that can be missed in a curriculum concerned with inculcating bits of knowledge more often than with 'knowing'.

A syllabus tells what to teach, never how. There are many syllabi and many versions of what English is, but I know of none which can tell how to generate the magic between person and person that leads to meaningful work and deep understanding. It must be for the English teacher to discover *his* ways with *his* groups. As he lives, writes and reads he will gather a hoard of materials which are in part him, and which it will become his purpose to share with his youngsters. It must be for him to judge what and when and with whom he can seek support, listen to advice, watch others at work, bring into his lessons someone he trusts, share his difficulties with people who know the same situation and who won't take his worries lightly. No one will be able to produce a prescription that will make individuals in his class feel they matter to him, or that he is glad to be with them. These thoughts, therefore, are offered out of the experience of sharing English with mixed ability groups in the hope of contributing to that support which might help the teacher develop his own ways of working.

Each group will unfold itself in a new way. Early lessons will need to foster the growth of fairly close knowledge of individuals in the class. The teacher will need to do much watching and listening to know just how his children are asking him to respond. He will need to reveal something of himself to encourage the beginnings of trust and start the process of getting to know each other. Some sort of experience shared by the whole class will have to be there, at least in the early days, and then the time will come for

making provision for youngsters to work in small groups or
on their own. Lessons will have to cope with different depths
of involvement, variations in mood, changes in friendship
patterns. There will be various problems related to style and
shaping of written work, a variety of approaches necessary to
encourage reading. As relationships develop it will also be
necessary to move in close with individuals as their needs
surface.

In the early stages with a group it may be essential to draw
quite heavily on stimulus material. Some offerings will come
from one's own store, but it is worth while preparing support
by getting to know as closely as possible what is available
within the department, what is useful, what there is to fall
back on in emergencies. This could involve a lot of deliberate
reading, and I have listed some of the anthologies that I feel
are worth getting to know at the end of the chapter.

If some of the work we do in English depends on sensing
and moving with the needs of the children, if a lesson is to
move meaningfully in an unexpected direction, for the whole
class, or a few, or for one person, the teacher must be busy
himself creating breadths and depths in his own personality.
His concern for his own growth will bring additions to the
hoard of ideas, novels, poems, short stories, experiences,
anecdotes which for him hold truth and meaning, secrets and
mysteries. One's own reading and writing can create seeds for
youngsters' work, and who knows when they might be
needed? I think it is on this sort of preparation that the
quality of work in harmony with a youngster, and the
sparking of individual interests depend. At this level preparation has the chance to become more than planning the
boundaries to be reached in a certain length of time and can
begin to be about gathering starting-points.

Another kind of preparation involves looking for ways of
appreciating what life is for different youngsters in the class.
Most of us who teach have tasted little but success in the
educational system. It must, therefore, be difficult to
understand just what it feels like to be unable to perform in
the kind of way which always seems to gain acceptance and
reward. We need to become sensitive enough to see how
easily, in the most uncalculated ways, youngsters have their

inabilities rubbed in. 'I'm a bad 'un, sir,' said one girl to me, rather knowingly and sheepishly. She wasn't being impish, nor was she inviting me to test her statement. She had come to accept what she said as a fact about herself. By the time she was fifteen she was coming to terms with it by staying away quite often. When she was at school she could be caught smoking in the toilets with monotonous regularity — hiding rather than rebelling. She knew her place, and no doubt she had learned it through countless uncoordinated incidents in Maths and English and Science, and whatever else she wasn't very good at. It was almost inevitable. Not one of the people who taught her would have wished to hurt her, but we all confirmed her lack of status, and our lessons must have proved how bad she was. What could have been done to help her feel that she was valued and that there was a place for her in the group is not easy to see. But I am sure that the beginnings of an answer could only have been found through someone first trying to understand how she felt and looking for ways of showing interest in her as a person.

Children in Distress, Born to Fail and *Children Under Stress* are essential reading. Making a point of getting amongst youngsters where they talk together can help to flesh the reading. An occasional exchange of staff-room gossip for playground gossip can be refreshing. Break or lunchtime duties can become opportunities to be with youngsters as they relax. Visits to local youth clubs through contacting the youth leaders could fill in some background to youngsters' out-of-school life, create a place to talk and points to talk about.

Friendships often begin with a gift. At the first meeting it could be the enjoyment of a story — something as simple, undemanding and deeply rooted as that. I always find it useful to keep my bag full of things I know and like, and, not knowing each other, we can start from there. With a group new to the school — be they eleven or thirteen — we might begin with something from *The Goalkeeper's Revenge* by Bill Naughton: 'Seventeen Oranges', 'Skinny Nancy', or the title story. It might be right to sense some of the nervousness of being in a new school through 'Billy the Kid' by William Golding (from *Listening and Writing*, Autumn 1965), and draw on memories of a more familiar school environment. In 'The Great Leapfrog Contest' by William Saroyan (in a BBC *Speak* pamphlet, Spring 1968) Rosie Mahoney beats the boys' champion into the dust. Reading this could spark off talk about how the girls always outdo the boys, or take us into a conversation about street games or gang games from earlier days. I enjoy reading and if I can manage it so that the group enjoys being read to, we might then move on to the first chapter of *There is a Happy Land* in another lesson, and talk of friends and falling out and getting back together again. A serialised reading of the novel may follow, with ideas for writing drawn out as we go.

Finding common ground is important in getting to know a stranger. A visit to contributory schools can create a starting-point. The best time is, perhaps, in the summer term when youngsters are anticipating the move, and it can be even more valuable if the visit involves a meeting and conversation with one or two children who now appear in the new class. Meeting teachers at these schools is meeting part of the children's experience. Just as important is to take the chance of talking with the children and of discovering some of the real lore about who has status and who doesn't, who's cock of the school, who's a scapegoat, who's always in trouble, what anecdotes there are to tell about characters in the year group. The information in itself isn't important, although some of it might filter through into the memory and come to have significance later on. Getting youngsters to talk on their own ground is the important thing. A morning, an afternoon, a couple of free periods can set up a wealth of encounters which may be fruitful at a later time. Youngsters will want to remember the visit because they will need to find things in common with a strange environment, and in early days with a new school or a new teacher, reminiscence can help to put children at their ease.

Stories from *The Goalkeeper's Revenge* can hold eleven, twelve, thirteen year olds as a class, and they remain fascinating reading for some older pupils. Older groups experience this sense of a new start too, even if they are ready to make the swiftest judgements about how ordinary anything school might present them with is going to be. For them the right material might be found amongst the stories in *Late Night on Watling Street* or from collections of stories by Barstow or Sillitoe, an extract from *A Kestrel for a Knave* by Barry Hines, or Graham Greene's story 'The Destructors'. Material for this purpose needs to be entertaining, to have the flavour of a good tale about it, and to be offered just as that. I once tried to use 'The Destructors' at an early stage with a group, to stimulate discussion on vandalism. A fifteen year old lad answered one of my earnest questions with 'But it's only a story!' He placed it exactly for me as a story worth listening to, but not to be extrapolated into real life, as I was doing at this stage in my relationship with the class. Discussion folded. I set a token piece of written work and left the real experience of the lesson to be simply the reading. This took its place along with the other pieces I shared with the class and helped prepare the ground for a serialised reading of *A Kind of Loving*, which I edited to focus entirely on Vic and Ingrid.

At another early lesson, writing books will be given out and youngsters will fill in their names. Someone might have difficulty even with this, and it will be important to pick that up very quickly. Some unobtrusive help may save a good deal of embarrassment and may help to set up a comfortable beginning for continuing help. A straightforward writing task will give an opportunity for observing how different youngsters begin to cope. The subject could be close to a story that has been offered, or it could be picked up from what the story has led the class to talk about. This will be the first request for them to reveal something of themselves, and they will need to be put at their ease if they are young and new to the place. More seasoned groups will obviously need less settling in, but there will be opportunities for breaking the ice — an offer of a pen where someone is without, reassurance for someone who wants to make sure they're doing the right thing — the opportunities are there to be seen and taken. Trust doesn't come quickly or because it is needed. There is a temptation to hurry things, particularly if the teacher needs a response from his group more urgently than they need to respond to him. You wouldn't let a stranger lead you towards an uncertain destination, and you would

only trust someone you felt safe with. It is only right to
allow the process of coming to know one other its own time.

An introduction to various working situations would be
appropriate at this stage. My first lesson with a group of
fourteen year olds in a South Yorkshire mining community
had caused me a few worries. This middle year in the
thirteen-sixteen span had struck me as the most effervescent
and most difficult to handle. I had been used to a fairly quiet
rural school, and I was unsure how I would tackle making
relationships in this very different environment. I decided to
offer a reading from *A Kestrel for a Knave*. There would be
no written work or questions. It was a thirty-five minute
lesson, and hopefully I could set up something to lead us into
written work for the double lesson on the following day. I
rode hints about a previous English teacher who 'couldn't
keep us under control, sir', and the myth that they were 'the
worst class in the school', and that we only mess about.' A
group of lads round a table just in front of my desk were
making the running whilst most of the rest of the class
seemed to watch with interest. I fell in with their good mood
and when they saw I was to read from *Kes*, the lads made
exaggerated efforts to get everyone quiet, as if to offer me a
chance of doing something interesting. The lesson went well
and the group enjoyed the opening pages of the book. But I
made the mistake of attempting to keep things at that pitch.
There were requests for more of the book next time I met
the class, and instead of providing them with something more
organised to hold their enthusiasm in this direction for
another time, I reproduced more of the same. We enjoyed
ourselves for a time, but the energy couldn't be sustained for
ever, and soon we were left directionless. I hadn't backed up
the work with *Kes* through other activities which could take
us forward as the initial impetus of coming together failed.
The youngsters were finding out what my tricks of the trade
were and I was finding out little about them individually.
Perhaps I was too concerned to have things go well in the
short term, perhaps getting over the first plunge was too large
in my mind. Whatever the reasons for the way I shaped these
early lessons, I put myself in a rut. English became my
reading to them and then drawing ideas for writing from

what I had read. The regularity of it was boring. I lost them for a long while, and really had to wait for my second year with them to come to a working relationship that I could use properly.

Activities for the whole class, apart from sharing a story, might include tackling suggestions for writing, following a duplicated extract from *Kes* or *Joby*, *The Bonny Pit Laddie* or *Walkabout* — each of which could be serialised. The class could be introduced to an anthology such as *Dragonsteeth* and asked to browse through and pick out work they like, to share it with others. Whilst this is going on, one is free to move from one cluster of readers to another, to suggest poems and pictures to look at, to engage in various conversations. Another possibility is to present a straight-forward choice of titles for written work, to look for individuals who may find none of the alternatives right, to talk with them to find something more appropriate. Bit by bit the idea of writing out of one's own thoughts might become part of the fabric of the lessons.

Group work could be introduced through a play-reading — 'Five Green Bottles' in *Family and School* goes well. Once groups have had a chance to read it, and perhaps act it out amongst themselves, the class could be drawn together for a dramatisation with each group putting forward someone who has had a chance to look at a particular part. Cups and saucers, knives, forks, a frying pan, radio, tablecloth, newspaper, spectacles, flat cap and envelopes will help the occasion. Groups might reform in a subsequent lesson to develop scripts of their own. If the atmosphere is right and some good material emerges, it may be possible to share some of the scripts with the class. 'The Mating Season', 'Don't Wait for Me', 'The Day Dumbfounded Got His Pylon' (in *Worth a Hearing*) 'Zigger Zagger' plays in *Conflicting Generations*, *Billy Liar*, Pinter's Dialogues, printed with *A Slight Ache* — which itself opens with a breakfast scene that a couple of people who have a real inclination for acting could well take on.

An introductory session with the class on Magazines, collecting on the board the different titles they are familiar with, some examples of the different interests catered for on

the station book stall, could lead to groups based on common
interests forming to produce magazines of their own.
Scissors, paste and old magazines will be needed, together
with sugar paper for covers, plain and lined paper for
illustrations and text. Michael Marland's *Following the News*,
relevant chapters from *Reflections* and *Language in Use* will
be useful for reference; as well as ideas for exploring — say —
related issues in advertising, censorship, or for comparing
newspapers. Headlines could be cut out of papers and stuck
at the top of sheets of writing paper, ready for someone to
compose an article. Issues to be explored could be written
down on work sheets or work cards, with follow-up tasks.

After looking at the Heath Robinson machines in *Things
Working*, or the inventions in Edward de Bono's *The Dog
Exercising Machine*, the class can move to individual efforts
at designing machines for incredible purposes (a fly-disposal
machine, a poem-making machine, the most gruesome
waking-up machine conceivable). A few ideas must be on
hand for any children who can't get their imaginations
working. Then there's the possibility of getting together with
the largest sheets of paper you can find and the most
ingenious ideas they can come up with. There will be much
intricate explaining to be done when a group introduces you
to the complexities of how their machine works. The
situation affords much scope for watching and listening to
youngsters. It is the sort of activity that can catch on
quickly, and can prove to be something youngsters want to
go back to again.

There needs to be room for one activity to grow into
another. Vic's bus journey to work on the first morning back
after an eventful Christmas (*A Kind of Loving*, Chapter 2)
may be used to stimulate some writing. If the class gathers
interest, the ground may be fertile for further readings. When
I use this novel again, I shall make sure that I have a number
of copies close at hand for I know now that some people will
want to take it away to read for themselves. Questions set on
the passage from *Joby* where the boy became involved in his
first theft have led to a serialisation of the whole novel. With
younger children, talking points and ideas for writing can be

drawn from Dick's interview with the Headmaster about his brother's truancy, or from the adventure down the old shaft. The strange discovery in an old rubbish tip in *Stig of the Dump* by Clive King may draw out memories of real adventures, of dens and secret hiding-places. Games with the Anglo-Saxon riddles from *The Earliest English Poems* or *Voices I* may lead to a reading of Rosemary Sutcliffe's *Dragonslayer* accompanied by collecting writings and drawings on the Beowulf theme. Ian Serrailler's version of the Beowulf story in *The Windmill Book of Ballads* should be available too. But in terms of developing the working relationship between the teacher and individuals in his class, it may be more important to have an enjoyable reading of *Walkabout* one lesson and writing from pictures of winter the next. I'm sure that it is the relationship between the teacher and his youngsters which offers the most important continuity of all.

Time will be needed in lessons to cope with different paces of working and different levels of involvement in a particular piece of work. Someone in the class may need to pause over an idea because it comes at just the right time for him, whilst another may simply need to do the required writing and pass on. One may feel that another can fit in all that seems to be expected, whereas he can't. Does he leave a piece unfinished and move on? Does he add one more to a backlog of incomplete pieces, with his real problems largely untouched? Does he avoid getting down to it at all? Another may find ideas of his own beginning to germinate, and will need time for them to develop. Above all, there must be room for pieces of work to be properly developed. Having put ideas and work, experiences and words in the air, the teacher must organise rooms for things to both settle and ferment, for youngsters to attend to the quality of what is to be said.

It has to be done bit by bit. The different paces of working will create opportunities for starting dialogues with individuals. As someone finishes there is the chance of looking at what he has done with him, of fathering some points of contact, of beginning to generate the feeling that a piece of writing can matter, that there are depths to be explored. Books and magazines should be at hand for other youngsters to take up and browse through, for it is never possible to deal with everyone meaningfully in this way in any one lesson. A session could be used specifically for completing work: the idea of 'finishing off for homework' may well be unhelpful because you are never there to take up the threads of the piece at the time when your response is most important and perhaps most effective. Reading may well become a dominant feature in these lessons to help create the atmosphere of on-going work. Gradually these working sessions can become the time when individuals can follow their own ideas for writing, find a special interest, be put in touch with a particular author or a particular topic. It will be the time when Ian will produce his piece of writing for me to read, and be able to expect a conversation to follow at a convenient moment.

Some people take readily to having time for themselves in lessons, others take much longer to develop work of their own, and some never do so. A background of set work — suggestions, possibilities embodied in the materials — must be there so that youngsters opt *into* their own work rather than *out of* whatever else is going on. In addition to collecting books and magazines, it is useful to build up a collection of cards, specifically written with people in the class in mind; these simply set out ideas, titles, situations, brief outlines of written work. One can write for particular individuals, touch on topics that may have emerged from conversations, offer thoughts which have particular meaning for oneself, include ideas that are appropriate in the whole context of the group's lessons, and maintain the element of choice and self-direction which belongs to a working session like this. With some groups this becomes the basic working pattern, but each class needs to settle in its own way.

Individual work is often most fruitful, the most elusive and difficult to support of the elements in work in English. So, finally, I would like to look at some pieces written by young people of fourteen and fifteen in a mixed ability group with which I am currently working. I have known the group for almost a year, although I did meet one or two of them two years ago in their final term at middle school. For their first year here, in the thirteen-eighteen High School, they were

taught English by a supply teacher who left suddenly, and I
picked them up just before the summer break.

The first piece is by Bill, who with his mate, Keith, shared
an easy partnership as the joint cocks of their Middle school.
Both have strong personalities, and both enjoy considerable
status amongst their peers in the class. In the first three
months that I taught the class, Bill's pieces of writing had
been short, perfunctory, and completed as a matter of course
without any real involvement. His thinking went much
deeper than his writing showed. He was swift to offer
imaginative solutions when we were looking at Anglo-Saxon
riddles, when many others in the class were puzzled or had
switched off. He could handle an argument and develop
points in discussion very perceptively. I came to believe that
the snippets he wrote were gestures in response to work I had
set, which mostly left him cold. I talked with him a good deal
and tried to let him sense my belief that there was much of
value to come in his writing, much more than was there so
far. Eventually he decided to see what he could achieve and
produced this:

A Dream of Life

The sun doth rise to the East over yonder mountain,
revealing rays of sunlight, producing shadows of bliss
among the gently flowing forest of trees and mingling
rivers, dazzling the sunbeams away. But there is a place
deep at the bottom of the valley where no sunlight
penetrates — the bewitched castle.

For almost a century the castle has laid under a cloak of
darkness. But up to this present day no human being had
set eyes on this castle of darkness for upon a century.
Today was the day that a certain young couple decided to
take a boat down a river for the day. It was while they
were on the river that they spotted the dark and eerie
castle and decided to take a look around. It was as though
the castle was pulling them towards it, but the girl, for
some reason, was very scared to go near the darkened
castle. The boy was as though he was in a trance. The girl
was starting to cry in amination of what lay in the castle.

As her tears fell on the ground, the tears made the darkened ground flush into green and lush grass and the greenness and freshness began to make the castle spring back to life, and music and laughter sprang from the castle walls. But as the couple drew nearer, a guard sprang out at them. My eyes opened. It was just after daybreak now and the rays of sunbeams filled the valley. Ah well, I must get back home.

I responded with the feeling that I was sharing a meaningful vision, and that Bill had broken through with this piece. We didn't discuss what it all meant — we both knew and saw enough to sense the depth of what he had written — I simply asked if I could have a copy for myself. We looked at some spelling and punctuation, touched on the content where we needed to confirm our understanding, and Bill wrote it out for me. More ideas grew from this piece and he followed it up with pieces called 'A Taste of Nature', 'Voodoo', 'Death or Death', 'Space and the Unknown' and 'Stonehenge'. This last piece came from some set work I did with the whole class which fitted with his drift — the only title not of his own making. After a number of weeks we came back to 'A Dream' and talked further, mainly because Bill wanted to write out his best work in a file. This time we ventured to explore the word 'amination'. I had chosen not to mention it before, not wishing him to feel uncomfortable about creating a word that had its own palpable meaning anyway. He confirmed it meant a kind of apprehension, not as strong as fear, although in that direction, but more mystical. I asked him to look at the last sentence which I felt wasn't quite right, if it was seeking to get to that feeling of waking from a dream to a less real world. A week or two later he had finished writing up the pieces he valued, and I noticed he had replaced the last sentence with: 'My eyes opened. Rays of sunbeams hit my eyes, as though blinding me from my dreams.' Later, when more has passed between us, we may come back again and talk more closely about the meaning of what he has written. At the moment the meaning is felt and understood. It is important for him to move on and avoid dwelling too much on what he has achieved so far. We have picked up the idea of

a search or a quest. I spent five minutes outlining the story of
Gawain and the Green Knight to him, and left him pursuing
the idea of a quest, a man's search for himself and the value
of his way of life in the Gawain setting. He is not yet ready
to tackle Brian Stone's verse translation of the poem but that
is what I shall move towards, and perhaps this will help to
start him reading, which he rarely, if ever, does. I noticed at
the end of the lesson in which I had set him off on this idea
that he had written three or four lines, starting with
something about Arthur's Court. Given time he may write
something, but that may mean that the idea is wearing thin
and that we need to look for an entirely different area of
work. We can only wait and see.

The conditions for fruitful individual work need careful
nurturing. The qualities in a youngster's writing which come
genuinely from himself will always be shy and hesitant. It is
rarely politic to expose one's real self to criticism, and if
English lessons are to be about finding space to say things
one really means, there must be a basis of confidence and
trust so that there is little fear of seeming foolish. When I
come across a piece of writing that is particularly meaningful
to me I may ask the author if I can have a copy. Usually I
have found that when youngsters sense the genuineness of a
response to their work, they are pleased to make a gift of it.
There is a power in being able to give something of value, and
it is important for a youngster to feel this.

Stuart could easily be put off writing. He knows he can't
spell or punctuate too well, and he is at a time in his life
when he must be weighing up the value of putting effort and
energy into a style of life which won't bring him much
success. And yet this is not an unusual piece from him:

The Stones

It was early, the clouds shadowed the stones. The dew
turned it into the shivering lake, but it was frosty. The
hillside blazed, the sun shone brightly, and the stones
shadowed giantly large and strong. A pigeon caught the
light, making it look a large unknown bird, but its coo let
its weakness out. Now the sun was bright and the shade of

the stones was damp and cold. The shadows seemed to
stretch for miles.

As a class we had looked at the opening picture in
Dragonsteeth of shadows cast by the stones at Stonehenge. I
had some pictures and information about other ancient
monuments — Avebury, Silbury Hill, Maiden Castle —
principally from a very readable book called *Exploring
Prehistoric England* by P. J. Helm. This piece was a response
to a suggestion I had made about imagining Stonehenge at
dawn. Stuart rarely has ideas of his own which he wants to
pursue in preference to what I suggest, although he doesn't
always find my ideas of interest. But he does need to have
the opportunity to write like this, and to have his achievement recognised. My individual work with him involves the
two of us getting together over some of the mechanics of his
writing, and sharing some of his successes with words. I have
still to discover, however, what it is that might fire him.

One Wednesday afternoon, while I was at the blackboard, I
noticed the look on Jackie's face. We were all squashed into a
working area adjacent to the library, and Jackie was sitting
close to the board. When there was room for an aside, I half
whispered to her, so that only she and her friend could hear,
'Are you bored?' She knew it wasn't an accusation, but
rather a gesture of sympathy. She nodded and said 'Yes', so
that only I and her friend could hear, and I went on with my
blackboard work. The following week I took her and the
friends she usually sat with on one side at the beginning of
the lesson. I had decided that they were ready to try
something entirely on their own. We went into the library
and I said I thought they were ready to attempt something
which I knew was quite difficult. I described how, sometimes, when I want to think or write, but am not quite sure
what I want to write, I may just set off on an ordinary idea
and pursue it until I begin to see what I really need to be
writing about, and gradually the piece takes shape. I said that
I wanted each one to think alone, in the quiet of the library,
away from the rest of the class, and come up with the thing
each needed to write. I left them to it. I was ready to accept
that nothing might come of it, and nothing tangible did, that

time. In fact, a teacher had come through the library and told them off for messing about when they should have been working, although they were really coming to terms with failing to reach what I had sent them to discover. But an idea, a possibility, an expectation had been planted. They were reassured by my readiness to go along with the fact that nothing had been possible this time, and the idea remained a serious one with them. Over the next week or so Jackie worked on this:

Emptyness

Why was I born into such a cruel world where no one cared, no one understood. The lonely nights spent between the same four walls night after night.

Nine chimed and lights were called. Now layed in darkness and no one to speak to except the spiders and noisy rats which kept me company during the long, dismal nights. After a busy day I soon fell asleep. The next thing I knew was breakfast was waiting. The doors creaked open, and the noise of moving feet echoed through the iron walls. Breakfast consisted of porridge and weak tea, followed by a day's hard work of scrubbing floors, and being watched by beady eyes.

Led back to our rooms, I thought for the first time of Pete. Bang, the doors were locked behind me again. And the same four walls appeared in front of me. That night I decided. Pete wouldn't wait for me, why should he after what I done to him? The next night when supper was over and lights were called out, I decided to end my troubles. I crept out of bed and rolled the mattress up and there, shining in the dark, was a knife. A cold shiver ran through my body, I began to wonder whether it was worth it, then I felt a trickle of blood on my wrist, then the room started to go round and

> round
> and
> round
> and
> round.

This piece seemed to catch a sort of sadness that was about her, but I didn't know Jackie very well, and we had never beaten a path between us that made it possible for us to talk meaningfully. Pete seemed real to me, but I know nothing of who he might be, or what he might mean. Perhaps the boredom I had noticed the week previously was not entirely to do with my lesson, but rather bound up with a whole complex of feelings and impulses she might have been experiencing. It was not for me to inquire about this and so, on the one hand I had a piece of writing from Jackie which had a great deal about it, to which I felt I must make a serious response, and on the other I had to respond without making her feel that she had said too much, if something of her real feelings were close to the surface. I think I said something like, 'You must have felt pretty fed up when you wrote this.' She gave me the impression that perhaps there was something of herself in it somewhere, and we talked for a short time about her mood. I tried to avoid leaving spaces in the conversation where she would feel either that she ought to talk about herself or support a silence. Then I moved on to look at spelling, punctuation, shaping; I took the occasion to be a possible starting-point for further work, and I wanted to work with her for longer than the time in which we could support a conversation about the substance of what she had written. She needed technical help, and we could also then slip into more securely defined roles and do a straightforward job together. This took place some weeks ago. I know nothing more about her personally — nor is it my province to know more. But we have begun to make the path between us.

Angela has started reading *Far from the Madding Crowd* — perhaps she saw the film on television. She finds it a stretch, but so far has stuck to it. Her writing shows some preoccupation with war. I have given her Wilfred Owen's poems to look at. As yet I am not sure whether she ought to pursue the Hardy or the war theme. Graham has started to be absorbed by *Pincher Martin* by William Golding, after trying *The Spire* and finding it too difficult. I ought to find a copy of *Lord of the Flies* for him for when he has finished *Pincher Martin*. Mark has taken to *The Time Machine* but he will need pushing to finish it. There is a group of girls who are

becoming increasingly disenchanted with school and I know
they see little point in what I press them to do in lessons. I
need to search for a way through there. The class is a rich
mixture of different people, full of surprising talents, full of
the magic that is there in all ordinary people. Each group has
its own gifts, its own magic.

REFERENCES
General Suggestions

M. Alexander (trans.) *The Earliest English Poems* Penguin
  Books 1966
Stan Barstow *A Kind of Loving* Penguin Books 1962
  Joby Corgi Books 1973
P. Blackie (ed.) *Things Working* Penguin Books 1970
A. Bradley (ed.) *Worth a Hearing* Blackie Student Drama
  Series 1967
A.B. Clegg and B. Megson *Children in Distress* Penguin Books
  1968
P. Doughty *Language in Use* Edward Arnold 1971
Graham Greene 'The Destructors' in *Twentieth Century
  Short Stories* D.R. Barnes and R.F. Egford (eds.) Harrap
  1959
F. Grico *The Bonny Pit Laddie* Oxford University Press 1960
Willis Hall and Keith Waterhouse *Billy Liar* Blackie Student
  Drama Series 1966
P.J. Helm *Exploring Prehistoric England* Robert Hale 1971
B. Hines *A Kestrel for a Knave* Penguin Books 1969
R. Jenkins 'Five Green Bottles' in *Family and School* David
  Jackson (ed.) Penguin Books 1970
Clive King *Stig of the Dump* Puffin Books 1965
M. Marland *Following the News* Chatto 1967
M. Marland (ed.) *Conflicting Generations* Longman 1968
J.V. Marshall *Walkabout* Peacock Books 1963 (first published
  as *The Children* by Michael Joseph 1959)
Bill Naughton *The Goalkeeper's Revenge* Heinemann New
  Windmill Series 1967
  Late Night on Watling Street Longman 1969
Harold Pinter *A Slight Ache* Methuen 1961
I. Serrailler *The Windmill Book of Ballads* Heinemann 1962
B. Stone (trans.) *Sir Gawain and the Green Knight* Penguin
  Books 1959

R. Sutcliff *Dragonslayer* Puffin Books 1966
K. Waterhouse *There is a Happy Land* Longman 1968
P. Wedge and H. Prosser *Born to Fail* Arrow Books 1973
E. Williams (ed.) *Dragonsteeth* Edward Arnold 1972
S. Wolff *Children Under Stress* revised edn. Pelican Books
   1973

Anthologies
D.R. Barnes (ed.) *People and Diamonds* (four books) Harrap
   1963
   Short Stories of our Time Harrap 1963
D.R. Barnes and R.F. Egford (eds.) *Twentieth Century Short
   Stories* Harrap 1959
Stan Barstow *The Human Element* Longman 1969
T. Belton *Slings and Arrows* Blackie 1966
B. Bennet, P. Cowan and I. Hay (eds.) *Spectrum* (two books)
   Longman 1970
M.G. and P. Benton (eds.) *Touchstones* (five books) English
   University Press 1968
E.L. Black (ed.) *Nine Modern Poets* Macmillan 1966
S. Clements, J. Dixon and L. Stratta (eds.) *Reflections*
   Oxford University Press 1963
S. Clements, J. Dixon, L. Stratta and R. Mayne (eds.) *Things
   Being Various* Oxford University Press 1967
C. Copeman and J. Gibson (eds.) *As Large as Alone* Mac-
   millan 1969
C. Downing *Russian Tales and Legends* Oxford University
   Press 1956
D. and E. Grugeon (eds.) *Poemcards* Harrap (three different
   collections of poems and pictures on laminated cards)
D. Grugeon and M. Wolman (eds.) *Happenings* Harrap 1964
D. Holbrook (ed.) *Plucking the Rushes* Heinemann 1968
   Story (three books) Cambridge University Press 1962
F. Inglis *One of the Family* Ginn 1971
D. Jackson *Springboard* Harrap 1970
D. Jackson and D. Pepper (eds.) *Story* Penguin Books 1973
R. Mansfield *Subjects of Inquiry* Blackie 1967
R. Mansfield and I. Armstrong (eds.) *Every Man Will Shout*
   Oxford University Press 1964
H.L.B. Moody *Facing Facts* Blackie 1966

T.H. Parker and F.J. Toskey *Themes to Explore* Blackie 1970
(a series of separate anthologies on themes such as *On
Being Alone, Animals in Captivity, The Adolescent*)
C. Parry (ed.) *Leopards* Cambridge University Press 1972
(three series of individual short stories by a wide range of
authors, in paperback)
R.H. Poole and P.J. Shepherd (eds.) *Impact* (two books)
Heinemann 1967
Albert Rowe *People Like Us* Faber 1965 (Muriel Spark's
'You should have seen the mess' can be a huge success)
A. Sillitoe *A Sillitoe Selection* Longman 1968
G. Summerfield (ed.) *Junior Voices* (four books) Penguin
Books 1970
Voices (three books) Penguin Books 1968
Penguin English Project, including:
Creatures Moving 1970
D.Ball (ed.) *Other Worlds* 1971
P. Blackie (ed.) *Things Working* 1970
D. Jackson (ed.) *Family School* 1970
E. Rowlands (ed.) *Ventures* 1971
G. Sanders (ed.) *I Took my Mind a Walk* 1971
B. Vance (ed.) *Being Born and Growing Older* Heinemann
1972
In and Out of Love Heinemann 1972
E. Williams (ed.) *Dragonsteeth* Edward Arnold 1972
People Edward Arnold 1970
BBC Publications *Listening and Writing* and *Speak* pamphlets
often contain useful material, and the summer edition of
Books, Plays Poems is often a good poetry anthology in
itself.

Suggestions for reading
A. Adams *Team Teaching and the Teaching of English*
Pergamon 1970
D. Barnes, J. Britton and H. Rosen *Language, the Learner
and the School* Penguin Books 1969
G. Barnfield *Creative Drama in Schools* Macmillan 1968
Edward Blishen *Roaring Boys* Thames & Hudson 1955
This Right Soft Lot Thames & Hudson 1969
Margaret M. Clark *Reading Difficulties in Schools* Penguin

Books 1970

A.B. Clegg *The Excitement of Writing* Chatto 1964

J. Dixon *Growth through English* Oxford University Press 1967

K. Gibran *Sand and Foam* Heinemann 1927

J.W.P. Gruger *Lost for Words* Penguin Books 1972

M. Hourd *The Education of the Poetic Spirit* Heinemann 1949

M. Marland *Towards the New Fifth* Longman 1969

G. Owens and M. Marland (eds.) *The Practice of English Teaching* Blackie 1970

G. Summerfield *Topics in English* Batsford 1965

G. Summerfield and S. Tunnicliffe (eds.) *English in Practice* Cambridge University Press 1970

4 French
Tony Warnes

I suggest the real reason why Language teachers do not, in general, look forward to mixed ability classes is that they will be faced, perhaps for the first time, with children traditionally considered unsuitable for such a demanding discipline. Foreign languages have become a sort of reserved occupation where the brightest and the best strive for standards of excellence far beyond the reach of most of their peers. The problem in most subjects is to tailor the work to fit the child; in French it is the reverse. A process of elimination hastens to consign the unchosen to Art and Woodwork rooms, leaving the way clear for the unimpeded progress of the gifted to 'O' level and beyond. The Language Department becomes the embattled stronghold of unashamed academicism, the rightful guardian of those standards now threatened by this Gadarene rush to mediocrity, the last refuge of the gentleman scholar!

I would, under pressure, admit to a degree or two of exaggeration in such a diatribe. Nevertheless, this view of the situation is not all that far removed from opinions currently echoed in many quarters, for one reason or another. It would be more helpful if people seriously concerned with the rôle of Modern Languages were to look forward to the abundant opportunities for experimentation inherent in an expanding situation. Better to welcome the chance to examine course content, to develop new techniques of presentation and to re-assess the place of Modern Languages in the curriculum, than to choose to pursue unproductive and divisive policies in defence of a position tenable only on frankly élitist grounds.

In a Comprehensive School with an annual intake of two hundred plus pupils, the Head of Modern Languages is, in the main, faced with three possibilities, each with its associated advantages and problems. If the school is streamed rigidly from the start he will have to hope that the criteria used have some relevance to future performance in a subject new to most of its practitioners, a remarkable example of the triumph of hope over impossible odds. If the setting system is used, then presumably the children will be taught in unstreamed classes for some considerable time, before any sort of examination can furnish statistics reliable enough to indicate exactly how their future exposure to language work should be ordered.

If we pause here to examine the raison d'être of these two systems, they are both based on the premise that it is more profitable to teach children of a like ability in any given class. The work to be covered by any group of pupils can be graded to suit their proven abilities, and everyone can move at his or her own pace. A transfer system between the groups ensures mobility and the competitive element encourages a high level of commitment. There are some questions which we ought to ask ourselves, however, before we opt for such procedures in Language teaching. Is it desirable, or even possible, to divide up Language work according to some nebulous difficulty quotient, especially in the early stages? What certainty is there that the allocation to suitable class groupings will not contain such a high percentage of error as to negate any supposed benefit? Why impose an artificial ceiling on the expectations of both teacher and taught? What happens to relationships on any level in a totally mobile situation? Who teaches the lowest streams? What happens to the child considered unfitted for Language work? In whose interests is the scheme worked, the child's or the teacher's?

The third possibility is to take advantage of the mixed ability situation and to make full use of its inherent strengths and freedoms. The main strength is that each Form is a self-contained unit with its own character and aspirations; it is no longer a rung in a ladder, only too conscious of the heights above it and the depths below. It is free to pursue its enquiries in a spirit of cooperation, not competition, as there is no longer any need to establish a top and a bottom with consequential penalties. Just as, in a streamed situation, the top Form did well partly because it was the top Form, so, in an unstreamed situation, every Form is equally capable of performing well, if this is what its teachers expect and require of it.

The eternal problems do not just disappear simply because different arrangements are made. We will always have the slow learner with us, posing for the Language teacher in particular the crucial problem of communication. In a class with widely differing abilities, how do you cater for this type of child and yet stimulate the highly gifted; and does the average child get ignored as the teacher attempts to reconcile the needs of the extremes?

Let us take it that, from now on, we have a mixed ability situation, in an 11-18 co-educational Comprehensive School, and that the main language to be taught is French. What follows owes more to evolution than to revolution, as it is a summary of the results of our excursions into the art of the possible at Campion School over the past seven years.

The first requirement is to have a clear idea of your aims and objectives and to make them realistic. If you take the decision to teach French to everybody you cannot pursue a straightforward academic course designed to meet the requirements of 'O' Level as quickly as possible; the long term objective for a few must not be allowed to distort the pattern of work laid down for the benefit of everybody. At the other end of the scale, pupils should not be allowed to drop French at any stage for purely negative reasons. The ideal seems to me to ask all children to do French for three years and, at the end of that time, for them to choose whether or not to continue with the subject on a CSE or 'O' Level course. After three years of expert help and guidance the children themselves are quite capable of assessing their own performance and prospects in the wide range of subjects which comprehensive schools can offer. They base their choices on three main contingencies; whether they are good at a subject, whether they like it and whether they need it for their future careers. In all respects it is a positive choice; pupils do not drop French, they choose to do something different. If pupils are allowed to drop out at any stage during the first three years, it seems to me absolutely essential that this must be a positive decision too. A real and meaningful alternative must be supplied, otherwise you are in danger of identifying a group of rejects, only too conscious of their status or, rather, lack of it. The social and educational ramifications of this can become quite devastating, especially in the Upper School. We expect all children to do English and Maths, irrespective of their performance in these subjects, so perhaps, as linguists, we should be prepared to employ our charges usefully for at least three years.

The most useful function we can perform is to give every child the opportunity of hearing good French and to develop his or her ability to respond in kind. This has always been the aim of the teacher of French, so much of what follows will probably already be standard practice in most schools. All I am saying is, why not teach good French to everybody, recognising that their individual response to the material provided will naturally vary quite substantially?

From the very start it has to be recognised that eleven year old children will not want to learn French just because it's good for them. They remain, for the most part, impervious to arguments concerning a European cultural heritage, flippant towards suggestions about continental cousins and the *entente cordiale*, and positively blank in the face of the Common Market. The point I am trying to make is that the impetus to learn the language springs largely from the teacher, and he cannot rely on a latent fund of self-interest to come to his aid. Children, in the main, will enjoy and use French if the teacher makes it an enjoyable and useful experience. The subject is about people talking to each other, and the most useful aid the teacher has is his own voice and presence.

The first few lessons in French are crucial in establishing the atmosphere required. If you are lucky enough to have a room of your own, make it as French as you can with posters, calendars and miscellaneous bric-à-brac. A couple of decorative wine bottles, previously drained in the line of duty, provoke a sympathetic reaction from the children, without unduly alarming parents. Tables are preferable to desks as they are more adaptable and less obviously scholastic.

The first lesson is based on 'Bonjour monsieur, mademoiselle, et comment vous appelez-vous?' This enables me to introduce the French habit of shaking hands, presents French as a practical and lively subject and teaches me the children's names! After a quarter of an hour or so I take five minutes to explain, in English, what we have been doing and what we are going to do next. In earlier years I would use no English for the first fortnight, relying on mime and the heartening response of the quick learner to carry us through. One day, however, I overheard a boy with a colourful turn of phrase confiding that he had been coming to my lessons for over a fortnight and had yet to understand a word. He obviously wanted to learn, had a natural flair for language and needed more careful guidance from his teacher. Thus, I make no apologies for this use of English, as it provides for the weaker child a necessary foothold in the shifting ground of the foreign language.

In the rest of the first lesson I introduce 'Qu'est-ce que c'est?' and the answer 'C'est un . . .' In the second lesson, after recapitulation, we move on to 'C'est une . . .', and I ask the children what they notice about the difference in sound. I even go so far as to write 'un' and 'une' on the board to underline the fact that this dichotomy is fundamental to French, that it doesn't exist in English, and that we shall have to proceed very carefully to avoid confusion. Every child hears the French I use and every child is encouraged, individually or in a group, to repeat it back to me. Obviously some move with more confidence than others, but it is important to involve the weaker ones, even if you have to give them considerable assistance.

In the third lesson 'le' and 'la' are introduced, along with prepositions like 'sur' and 'devant'. The rest of the first week is devoted to manipulating these simple skills on an active basis. Pupils take it in turn to put *le sac, le livre, le crayon, le stylo, sur, devant, dans, sous, la chaise, la table, le professeur, le pupitre* and then they ask the question 'Ou est le stylo (etc)?' You can then introduce 'Vous avez raison — Vous avez tort' for them to use as well.

Perhaps I should pause here to say that I regard it as a fundamental necessity to see these children once a day, every day. A little and often is the prescription if the treatment is to be effective, possibly because we work a forty-period week; I can foresee complications if thirty-five is the norm. You will also have noticed that, in these early lessons, a lot of time is spent in fairly formal class teaching, and I do not see how this can be avoided where the teacher is, as it were, the fount of all knowledge, muddy or otherwise. In a subject that is purely oral in the early stages and mainly oral later on, new material can effectively be introduced by the teacher addressing the whole class, and individualising the follow-up work, after the initial stimulus has been given to all.

In the second week we introduce verbs which can be easily mimed — *je prends, je mets, je regarde, je touche, j'ouvre, je ferme, je chante, je bois* (remember the wine bottles!). The teacher can use the imperative of the verb as a stimulus, or 'Qu'est-ce que tu fais/vous faites?' The children are also introduced to 'il' and 'elle', and this encourages them to watch and listen to their companions very carefully so that they, in turn, may answer the question 'Qu'est-ce qu'il/elle fait?'. I write 'il', 'elle' and 'je' on the board to make things flow more smoothly, but the emphasis is on getting the children to do something simple and to talk about it in the foreign language. This seems to me to be a very worthwhile goal to aim for and it is within the reach of everybody at this level.

At about this stage I introduce 'learning' games, simply because I have not yet found a more effective or quicker way of covering this sort of material. We do numbers, the days of the week and the months of the year by writing lists on the board, reciting them with great gusto as the words are erased one by one. It takes them back to their Junior School days and the nostalgia works wonders! It also means you can get the date written up every day as a matter of course, and enables you to introduce 'Quel âge as-tu?' and birthdays, and thence lead smoothly on to 'Quelle heure est-il?'

This is the pattern that is followed until halfway through the first term. The topic is introduced by the teacher to the whole class; their response is checked on a general, then individual, basis; activities help in the assimilation of the new material. Key words are written up on the board where such a procedure is deemed useful in underlining new material.

After half-term reading and writing are introduced in fairly quick succession. I usually write the first reading passage on the board, so that I can be certain it only contains words the children have heard several times over. When choosing a course book two things are of paramount importance; the reading passages must be short and they must be closely allied to an accompanying picture. Indeed, one sentence per picture is probably most useful at this stage. As what is happening is obvious, the problem of comprehension is alleviated and this allows you to concentrate on pronunciation. Most books have their own French questions based closely on the text, but with pictures, the range of questions you yourself can ask is greatly extended, covering such topics as numbers, colours, positions, clothes, weather, time, all the things you have dealt with previously. Again, children who have difficulty in reading should be encouraged to take part, even on a word to word basis. If the teacher accepts this as natural nobody will notice anything unusual. It is important to stop a child thinking he is making a fool of himself every time he opens his mouth to read, or you will quickly find yourself faced with a barrier not easily raised.

Taped courses are a useful aid, especially when used in a language laboratory. They should be used sparingly, however, as some children just do not like talking to tape-recorders, and others find difficulty in concentrating on a disembodied voice and always complain it is speaking too fast. We have an Audio Active system, which means the children cannot record their own voices, but they all get an opportunity to read or repeat French without feeling that everybody is listening to their mistakes.

After reading a passage and discussing it in French, we then dramatise it in groups. Generally speaking, these groups are self-regulating, but they can be manipulated by the teacher to achieve a workable balance. Many course books follow this procedure, supplying dramatic sequences of their own. I usually read through this with the children and we decide which bits to incorporate in our versions; the new material is written up on the board and each group uses it in its own way. The whole class discusses the merits of the various performances and it is noticeable that the over-riding virtue they soon learn to seek is comprehension. If they can understand the words then it is a success. This exercise teaches them the value of clarity of speech and how to make use of the French they accumulate as the weeks pass by.

The introduction of writing is a mixed blessing, so why introduce it? We do so because, for the majority of the children, there is no problem beyond one of spelling, resulting largely from unfamiliarity with the new material. The first writing we do consists largely of copying sentences from the board or out of a book; we check for the accuracy of the written word, and find that most children cope satisfactorily with this new skill. But, even at this stage, it becomes obvious that some children, say four or five in any class, are already experiencing severe problems with written French. If you wish to discover the extent of the real problem, then give the class a dictation consisting of three or four sentences they have heard and seen several times before. Collect in the papers, go through them carefully, and you will discover another half dozen children who will have great difficulty in producing written French on their own.

On the credit side, a lot of children welcome this chance to get to grips with the language in a more concrete form. Some very intelligent children, not extrovert enough to be wholly comfortable with oral French, need to manipulate the language in their own way and this presents them with an ideal opportunity to take control of the actual words and fit them into set patterns in their books. From the teacher's point of view, it gives him another variation to use, something else which will help two thirds of the children to get to grips with the language.

This still leaves us with the other third, and it is most important that they do not come to look upon French as a written subject which they cannot do. Words spoken in a foreign tongue disappear and can quickly be corrected; words written have an existence of their own; they lie there, evidence of rightness or wrongness, for all the world to see. If a child's written work is marked against some absolute standard of perfection, the weaker children will soon get discouraged and react accordingly. They know they have problems and, if by your attitude to their efforts, you merely confirm their fears, the position soon becomes hopeless for

both parties. For the first piece of written work a child does
for me he gets an 'A', the highest mark. Usually, it being the
first piece of written work and so something rather special, it
is carefully and conscientiously done, and provides me with a
standard against which to measure all his subsequent offerings. Each child is marked against himself, and the mark
which appears in his book reflects the effort judged to have
been put into the work being assessed. In my mark book
there are two columns; one for the mark appearing in the
child's book and the other for a more objective assessment of
the work done. But in the child's book we are interested in
progress, in encouraging the child to continue doing something he finds quite difficult.

There remains one other aid to discuss and then we will
have covered the pattern which holds true for the rest of this
first year. Obviously the range of topics suggested immediately by the classroom situation is somewhat limited. When
these have been exhausted we use filmstrips to give us the
immediacy so necessary if the language is going to come alive.
They can either be based on the course book or be quite
separate, just so long as they provide a lively and colourful
basis for extending vocabulary and creating interest. Usually,
the strips tell a little story and I take them through this in
French, giving each picture two or three sentences. I then ask
questions about the pictures, and the new vocabulary is put
on the board; coloured chalks come in handy here, red for
verbs, yellow for adjectives and so on, anything to reinforce
the point you are trying to make. We then go through the
story once more, with the children giving as much information, relevant or otherwise, about what is going on in the
pictures, and the new words are given great emphasis. The
final stage is to give the children, either on the board for
them to copy or on prepared Banda sheets, sentences in
which these new words are missing and then to get the
children to put in, hopefully, the right word from the list in
front of them. The next day, perhaps, the children can be
asked to present their own version of the story in dramatic
form, using as much of the new vocabulary as possible.

Assuming five lessons a week, the following pattern could
emerge. One lesson based on the film strips, mainly oral but

with a possibility of written work if required; one follow-up lesson, in which the new material is put to active use by the children; one reading lesson with an oral question and answer session at the end, followed in the next lesson by oral or written exercises on the same topic. As for the fifth lesson, we generally use it as revision time, in which we take a topic covered a fortnight or a month before and try to revitalise it.

Homework is put on an official basis after half-term in the first term. Until then the children have to request it and it is surprising how fervent some of their pleas are — halcyon days! It is set once a week and usually consists of either learning or writing French. Written homeworks have to be carefully explained, and it is advisable to start them in the lesson, so that you can see if it is going to serve any useful purpose. If most of the children are getting it wrong then abandon it before you run out of hair and red pens.

We do not set a formal examination in French at the end of this first year; it would not be a fitting summary of our aims and methods and so has no relevance at this time.

The weaker linguist can be catered for, but what about the really gifted ones? In oral work they can be asked the more searching questions. With written work they can be required to answer more questions or to help children with problems. They will write plays, cast them and produce them with terrifying efficiency. They will produce scrap-books containing mountains of unusual information about some aspect of French life and will deliver short lectures to their classmates on topics varying from why French fashions are so successful to why French footballers are not. Their work can be scrutinised for the slightest error and it must be tacitly understood that you expect good work of them and that nothing but their best is good enough. Children will progress at different speeds and be fully aware of this fact; this is natural. What is unnatural, and can place great strain on a situation, is for the teacher to imply that his prime concern is for the obviously successful pupil and that his efforts alone are worthy of praise.

In our school all pupils carry on with French in the Second Year, and the approach is very similar to the one laid down in the First Year, but with certain changes of emphasis. We do

more reading, sometimes for the pleasure of a good story and
sometimes to test comprehension. As the French becomes
more complicated some written or oral comprehension work
can be done partly or wholly in English. There are several
inexpensive short readers produced by publishers such as
Mary Glasgow & Baker, which children can read on their own
and you can quickly build up a library of such books.

The work on the film strips can be developed into
full-scale essay work this year. The pupils supply the French
and I write it up on the board, making the occasional mistake
to keep the academics on their toes. There are several ways in
which this can be developed. The passage can be read out two
or three times then all the verbs erased; the children can be
asked to learn it for homework and to reproduce it the next
day under guidance; sentences can be erased and used for
dictation purposes.

Individualised oral work can be a problem and possibly the
simple dramatic situations have been played out in the First
Year; nevertheless, I think there is still a place for them.
French monologues can be used, in which a child prepares a
speech about some aspect of his own life at home or at
school, or he may assume the identity of a postman or grocer
and talk about his imagined life. The other children then ask
him simple questions in French about himself and what he
does. This can be very effective, as it teaches the solo
performer to express himself coherently under pressure, and
gives the others an opportunity to ask rather than answer
questions in a thoroughly practical exercise.

The tendency in the Second Year can be for the lessons
themselves to become more complicated and for certain
things to be taken for granted. But, in a mixed ability
situation it is as well to decide what particular skill you wish
to develop in any particular lesson and then concentrate on
that, and though you, as the teacher, know how the lessons
inter-relate I think it is important that each lesson be a
self-contained unit as well, with a natural progression built in.
The lessons must exist for themselves and the amount
retained will vary from pupil to pupil; I think we must be
prepared to state the obvious every lesson, to remind children
constantly of the basic workings of the language and not to

take it as a personal insult if they do not remember these
things.

Certain grammatical points can best be made in a straightforward manner. Provided the issue is not clouded in
technical jargon, these lessons are quite popular. We think of
it as playing about with the language and treat it as a game,
the rules of which you must know before you can play and
enjoy it. Verb-endings are an obvious candidate for such
treatment. Divide the class into two teams, who take it in
turn to write the correct part of the verb in prepared
sentences on the board, with the option of changing the
other team's version if they think it is wrong. Competition
put to a useful end, but don't try and rig the result or you
will be lynched! Grammar lessons are useful and enjoyable
when part of a balanced diet.

Towards the end of this second year we do set a
reasonably formal examination. The children are told the
main areas to be covered, and most of the information they
require to do the work is to be found somewhere on the
paper. It lasts for one hour and it is deliberately designed to
take a good candidate longer than this. Everybody can do
something on the paper, but nobody does it all. This exam,
coming as it does after eighteen months of French, is mainly
for my benefit, a sort of self-assessment carried out for me by
other people. It shows which parts of the course have been
effective and which parts need attention. It is essential,
however, that it works to the benefit of the children too,
even those who find it difficult. I go through each child's
paper with him individually, and stress the things he got
right; we then apportion the blame for the disasters and both
of us promise to do better in future. The child does not see
any marks on the paper, there is no rank order published and
this helps to underline the fact that you are interested in
everybody's performance. Nobody sets out with the
intention of getting a bad exam result and the ordeal
demands some praise.

At the end of the Second Year I would concede that a case
can be made out for allowing certain children to drop the
subject. But again, I stress that the alternative offered must
be a viable one and regarded as worth while by both teachers

and children alike. If it is only possible to fit in a stop gap course, then I would far prefer to carry everyone forward into the Third Form. During the second term of this third year children choose the subjects which they wish to study in their final two years. French goes into this Option Scheme and the child, after full consultation with all interested parties, takes the final decision. Most, but not all, of the children base their choice on their future prospects at CSE and 'O' levels. It is important then, that during the third year some indication is given of the importance attached to written accuracy by the various Examining Boards. This means that more emphasis will have to be given to written work, but it must not be allowed to discourage the children who find this work difficult. They rightly complain that our grammatical demands are more stringent than those of our confrères who, I take it, teach in the native tongue!

By the end of the Third Year I like the children to have had a thorough grounding in all aspects of the Perfect Tense and to be reasonably conversant with the Imperfect. I do not want any other complication of structure of vocabulary, however, so we use a Second Year book which happens to cover this material in a suitable manner, Mark Gilbert's *Cours Illustré de Francais* (Book II). The exploitation of the material is very similar to the way we have been working in the previous two years and everything is fully prepared in a class situation before the individual is required to produce his own written French.

Three-stage work sheets can be prepared in advance to give practice in the skills you are trying to develop. Work sheet 'A' contains the assignment to be completed, with all the information necessary for its completion. Work sheet 'B' contains a similar assignment with selected areas of information. Work sheet 'C' has the assignment and no information at all. When dealing with the perfect tense, for example, 'A' would have 'Avoir' and 'Être' written out in full and all the relevant past participles: 'B' could have both auxiliary verbs and no participles, or vice-versa: 'C' would have no detailed information, just gaps in the passage where the verbs should be.

The children, working at their own speed, will complete

these sheets with varying success. A few may never make the transition from 'A' to 'B', whilst others will miss 'B' out completely and go straight to 'C'. Nevertheless, it means that quite complicated written work can be incorporated into the course at this stage without penalising any group of children.

Multiple-choice questions are yet another way of circumventing the writing barrier. The children select the right answer from a selection of three or four possibilities and, providing the alternatives are carefully worked out, the exercise can be quite a demanding one. Several publishers are issuing books containing work of this sort and I have found that children welcome them as an interesting variation.

Another course we have found very useful is the B B C 'Allons-Y' course. It consists of a series of tapes and booklets, again with a three-stage development pattern. First the child hears the passage while looking at the relevant pictures; then the tape is exploded and he reads the text in short sections; finally the storyline is dramatised, extra details are incorporated, but basically the same structures are practiced. It deals effectively with many points, notably object pronouns and the perfect tense. It is popular with the children because it is lively and interesting; the weaker ones can follow the story from the pictures and the abler ones are delighted to find that they can follow French which they have never seen or heard before with relative ease. I usually give a written comprehension in English on the final dramatised section and have found that the ablest candidates get it all right and even the weakest ones do quite well.

Longman's French Packs contain lots of information about France and the French, presented in an attractive and interesting way. They can all be used in the Third Form, but 'La Vie en France' or 'Le Pays de France' are particularly suitable. They are self-contained units, easy to use and highly informative. Children like using them and this includes the bright ones. So often this is the sort of material they would never see in a streamed situation, but which should be an integral part of what we are trying to do.

In February then the children all take an examination designed to test their ability to do French to external examination standards. Afterwards we go through the paper with the individual candidates and discuss their prospects. We advise, but the child has the final say and can continue with the subject even if we think examination success is unlikely. We have always stressed that it is the experience itself that is important and it is pleasing when the children think so too. We do not reject them at the end of three years but they may well choose to do something else.

On a technical aspect, the sort of examination question which does test what you have been teaching all year, and which can predict fairly accurately a child's future performance, is sometimes difficult to construct. This is the one we have found quite effective:

Read the following passage but do NOT translate it:

> Madrid
> dimanche
> le deux juin

Chère Maman,

J'y suis arrivé hier à quatre heures. Le voyage en avion de Paris à Madrid a duré une heure dix minutes et j'ai eu une vue splendide des Pyrénées. Mon hôtel est petit et situé dans une rue étroite; j'ai une chambre au premier.

Hier soir, je suis allé à un restaurant près de l'hôtel mais je n'avais pas très faim. Je me suis couché tôt et j'ai bien dormi. Ce matin, je me suis lavé, naturellement, et puis j'ai mis ma nouvelle chemise rouge, celle que tu m'as achetée aux Galeries Lafayette. Après avoir mangé mon petit déjeuner, j'ai fait le tour de la ville et puis j'ai trouvé ce jardin publique. J'ai décidé de m'asseoir sur un banc et de t'écrire.

> Jean

Answer the following questions in complete FRENCH sentences:

1 Qui a écrit cette lettre?
2 Est-ce qu'il a écrit à son père?
3 Ou est Jean?
4 À quelle heure est-ce que son avion est parti?
5 Quelle était la date de son arrivée en Espagne?
6 Est-ce que Jean est Espagnol?

 7 Qu'est-ce qu'il a vu pendant le voyage?
 8 Est-ce que L'Espagne est au nord de la France?
 9 Est-ce que Jean se trouve dans un grand hôtel anglais?
10 Est-ce qu'il a diné a l'hôtel, samedi soir?
11 Pourquoi n'a-t-il pas beaucoup mangé?
12 Comment savez-vous qu'il était très fatigué?
13 Pourquoi est-il allé à la salle de bain ce matin?
14 Qu'est-ce qu'il a mis?
15 Qui a acheté la chemise rouge?
16 Est-ce que Les Galeries Lafayette sont à Madrid?
17 Quand Jean a quitté l'hôtel ou est-il allé?
18 Qu'est-ce qu'il a enfin trouvé?
19 Ou s'est-il assis?
20 Qui va reçevoir cette lettre?

In the Fourth and Fifth Forms we do not divide up into C S E and G C E groups. Whenever possible we try to keep children with staff they already know, thus avoiding the problem of mutual adjustment to personality. It also saves time spent working out which mistakes are being made through carelessness, as opposed to those which need looking into more deeply. If you do this it is important to be able to match up the C S E and 'O' level Courses that you are following, so that any decision as to which to go for can be left until Christmas of the Fifth Year; you can always submit your own Mode III if problems of this nature arise.

A lot of C S E Boards are establishing a French Studies syllabus as an alternative to French itself. The emphasis is on the geography, history and culture of France, usually involving some sort of course work, but containing a good deal of language work as well. The oral side is kept, but the children are not expected to write in French, being restricted to listening to and reading the language and answering any written questions in English. The proportions are usually in the region of sixty per cent for background material, forty per cent for language work. We have had no experience of this type of course as yet, but for the child who is really involved in the first three years yet who has difficulty with written French, it does seem to offer a viable alternative, with the added incentive of examination success at the end of the course. It would mean making a definite choice at the end of the Third Form as to which course to follow, but this would perhaps be a small price to pay for the extra range and dimension gained by its introduction.

Returning to our current practice, the actual work we do in these two years is subject to exactly the same techniques as used in previous years. Written work is still carefully prepared beforehand, including essays, but I like these to be as personal as possible providing, as they do, opportunities for the really able candidate to go on display. Multiple-choice questions are becoming popular with several Examining Boards and, though ours do not use them, we still make use of them within the lessons.

The A E B gives twenty-five per cent of their marks for oral work and the E M R E B gives forty; this means that oral work remains an integral part of the Course and does not have to be regarded as pleasant but not essential. Most Boards have become more enlightened and dynamic in this respect than others, and this means the language teacher no longer has to compromise his educational beliefs and allow the dead hand of examination procedure to choke the life out of the living language.

Before I close I ought to mention the introduction of a second language. I would not expect everybody to take one, as this would corner a quarter of the while timetable for Modern Languages. It could go into the Option Scheme at the end of the Third Year, leading to 'O' Level perhaps in the first year in the Sixth Form. Or it could be offered at the end of the Second Year, not necessarily set against another subject, but taking a period here and there from various other subjects. Whenever it is introduced it would, to all intents and purposes, be self-selecting, as children who have real difficulty with French are unlikely to choose it. It would still be a mixed ability situation, but the problems posed by the lower end would not be so acute.

In this brief summary of the type of Five Year Plan we operate, I am only too conscious that I must have cut several corners and begged a few questions. I have not done this deliberately and hope that the reader can glean enough information about the possibilities offered by the mixed ability situation to have both the confidence and desire to exploit it. The alternative would seem to be to watch Modern Languages follow their Classical counterparts into some obscure niche of the timetable, of minor interest to a select few. I have taught for six years in streamed selective schools and for seven in an unstreamed all-ability school. The latter experience has been by far the richer one, with children and staff fully involved in uncovering the potentialities of the situation. I am convinced that French has been a valuable experience for several individuals who, in a streamed situation would not have been given the opportunity of developing, however, temporarily, this demanding skill. Those with the ability to manipulate language on a higher level have enjoyed sharing responsibility for setting the pace and establishing the tone of the lessons, whilst the children between these two extremes have been encouraged to experiment with the various skills inherent in the subject to discover whether these have any relevance to their future needs, in all senses of the word.

I would like to end by giving a list of books and material I have found useful. Unlike us, however, it is by no means fully comprehensive!

Course Books:	*Cours illustré de français*, Mark Gilbert, U.L.P. Longmans Audio Visual French

Other Useful Books

1st Year:	'L'arche de Noé' by G. Young, Arnold 'Les Duval' by A.M. Topping, Arnold 'French for Beginners', filmstrips, B B C
2nd Year:	*Bonnes vacances: Venez à Paris*, A.M. Topping, Arnold *Life in a French Town* D.L. Ellis, Harrap *Michel et le loup*, S.H. Miller-Jacob, Arnold
3rd Year:	*Voyage à Paris*, R. Leeson, Longmans 'Allons-Y', pamphlets and tapes, B B C
4th and 5th Years:	*Le petit Nicolas*, R. Goscinny, Longmans *Regardez et écrivez*, N.E. Mountjoy, Arnold *Passeport pour le passé*, N.E. Mountjoy, Arnold 'La vie en France'

'*Le pays de France*'
'*Histoire de France*'

The European Schoolbooks Catalogue is always worth consulting.

5 Mathematics
Peter Wilcox

Mathematics teaching was just beginning to settle down into a comfortable rut after the development of 'modern Mathematics', when the move towards mixed ability teaching groups started to gather momentum. Modern Mathematics had achieved a certain respectability and discussion over mathematical content and teaching methods was beginning to subside. However, under the impact of this latest trend many Mathematics teachers are forced once more to analyse their subject critically.

Unfortunately, not all mathematicians are so open minded. Many resist this new trend, seeing yet another erosion of academic standards. Others hold the opinion that mixed ability teaching in Mathematics is impossible, because of the nature of the subject. Others just ignore the trend and hope it will never reach them. But for whatever reason, Mathematics is one of the most intransigent subjects under the challenge of this trend. This is emphasised by the recent survey into mixed ability teaching conducted by the Assistant Masters Association; in their report entitled *Mixed Ability Teaching*, they state: ' . . . that Mathematics teachers in secondary schools were more reluctant than other specialists to adapt their approach and methodology to the needs of mixed ability groups'.

Much research has pointed to the bad effects of streaming in schools. Obviously Mathematics teaching cannot remain aloof from these findings. Although I have only been involved in mixed ability teaching for a short time, I am convinced of its advantages in the early years of Secondary School. However, to achieve the aim of effective Mathematics teaching to mixed ability groups a complete reappraisal of the subject, and of teaching methods is needed.

In my experience, for effective teaching there must be a

change of emphasis from class or formal lessons to an approach geared to the individual, with each child progressing at a rate appropriate to his or her ability. Many teachers, not only Mathematics teachers, are worried over this change. They are not only concerned over the preparation of suitable courses; one question often asked is: 'How do you manage to see each child in a class of thirty in a lesson lasting only seventy minutes?'

Before answering this question let us examine critically the previous situation. Teaching supposedly homogeneous groups, we would start by developing our topic by class discussion and after perhaps a quarter of an hour all but the brightest would have lost concentration. We would continue to develop our arguments, perhaps now boring some and confusing others. An exercise would then be set, and all the children except for the able would require help, very often at the same time on different points. At no time did we believe it necessary to see each individual child every lesson. It is exactly the same with an individual learning approach, but we also have the advantage that each child can progress at a suitable rate and not one falsely imposed by the teacher trying to pitch his lesson to the middle of the group. It is not often realised that even in an homogeneous group there is a tremendous spread of ability.

If the change is to be away from formal class lessons an alternative form of instruction must be found. To many teachers the obvious answer is work cards. If this method of instruction is to be followed a decision has to be taken on the structure of the work card system, whether to have a linear approach, in which cards are attempted sequentially, or a topic approach, in which the topics can be attempted in any order. Whichever approach is adopted, care has to be taken over the production of the cards to present the work in a logical order and in a way that it is easily understood by all abilities. This last point is important, since the children will spend the majority of their time working by themselves and a badly planned or written work card can lead to a chaotic situation with many children requiring help at the same time. It is better to have a large number of cards slowly developing the topic, rather than a few lengthy cards, when the pupil, especially the less able pupil, is faced with a daunting amount of reading and work on each one.

Not only methods, but the content of courses and aims must be reassessed. On the one hand the topics offered must appeal to the individual child and relate to his real world. The work must interest and stimulate the children's imagination and lead to a pleasure in mathematical activity. Particularly important is the need for the work to be such that it maximises the child's chance of success. On the other hand the work must develop Mathematical ideas and give a view of the internal relationships and structures of Mathematics. By a suitable choice of work we must try to develop reasoning powers and the ability to see mathematical pattern, both in space and number, and to apply it, we must also, not forget the need to develop certain skills and techniques. Previously, I feel, far too much emphasis was placed solely on the acquiring of certain skills.

Previously I taught in a Comprehensive School, organised along traditional lines, into three bands, and Forms were streamed in these bands. It was possible to see the bad effects of streaming indicated by research, such as the under-achievement of children in the lower forms of the top band, and the poor attitude of children in the lowest band. After experiencing this system I am far happier to be working in a mixed ability situation. However, my views and my teaching methods are continually being refined, and, although it is a far from a definitive statement on mixed ability teaching in Mathematics, I hope this account of our experiences at Radyr will be of interest.

On entry into Radyr, children are placed into six mixed ability Forms; most subject areas keep this mixed ability grouping at least for the first two years, and some even continue into Form Four. There is a flexibility in the timetable to allow subject areas to set, if and when they wish. Children requiring remedial help are extracted from only those subjects in which they have particular difficulties. In Mathematics this is often on the ratio of 3 children to a class of 32. Every effort is made to re-integrate the children into main stream lessons as soon as they have mastered their difficulties.

The school buildings are laid out in faculties, and in the Mathematics and Science Faculty the Mathematics Department has three rooms. These Mathematics rooms are slightly larger than the usual classroom, and have work-tops round their sides. Two of the rooms are grouped round a central project area, which is frequently used by individual children for independent work.

The school opened in September 1972, with only a fraction of the buildings completed, but fortunately the Mathematics rooms were in the completed section. The first year's intake consisted of approximately 550 children; forming First, Second and Third Years, coming to us not only from a number of Primary Schools but also from Secondary Schools, ranging from single-sex Grammar Schools to a very large Comprehensive. During our first year we not only had to face the problems of setting up mixed ability teaching, but we also had the problems of the widely differing backgrounds of our Second and Third Year pupils. Apart from the variations in their mathematical experiences, some having followed a traditional and others a very modern course, we also had to cope with differences of attitude, and deal with living in the middle of a building site for much of the year. On reflections it is a wonder that we survived that first year!

When the school opened the Headmaster indicated that he expected us to continue with mixed ability groupings at least for the first term. This was really being thrown in at the deep end. Unfortunately, as we were a new school with teachers being appointed from widely separated areas in England and Wales, there was very little opportunity for consultation over the setting up of mixed ability teaching, and so our first year tended to be one of assessment and experimentation. In fact, we are still refining our course and, hopefully, we shall continue to do so.

First, I had to decide on the content of courses, not only in our initial mixed ability years, but throughout the school. I was certain that a traditional approach, with its emphasis on skill acquisition, would not be suitable for the school as I saw it developing. I wanted a course which would stimulate the children's imaginations and interests, and would generate an excitement in Mathematics. Learning Mathematics must not just be the passive assimilation of techniques and skills, but the children must be actively involved in its development. The courses also had to be such that the children would be confronted with situations which would increase their chances of success, for the old maxim 'Nothing succeeds like success' is nowhere truer than in the teaching of Mathematics.

It would be impossible to find a set of textbooks which would completely encompass any set of objectives, but *The School Mathematics Project Main School Course* (published by Cambridge University Press) seemed to come closest to my ideal. This course also had the advantage that it would be possible to use it as a common course for the whole school, with extension to 'O' level through books X, Y and Z, and for the less able children higher in the school by the introduction of further materials, either topic books, such as the *Making Mathematics* series (published by Oxford University Press), or duplicated booklets produced by staff.

We were then faced with a decision as to how best to use this available material in the light of mixed ability groups. Initially, we tried giving class lessons, and we soon found the problems involved with this approach, particularly in Years Two and Three. We encountered difficulty in pitching a lesson and, particularly in Year Three, we were conscious of holding back the more able children while we laboured points with slow learners. This was clearly unsatisfactory, and we soon came to the conclusion that the only real solution was an individual learning situation, that some type of work sheet or assignment sheet was necessary. As you can imagine, the writing and duplicating of work sheets for all three years was a forbidding task; for this reason we decided to tackle each year separately. Since the problem of differing backgrounds magnified our difficulties in Third-Year classes we first concentrated our efforts on this year group.

We evolved a system of work sheets, assignment cards and class lessons. This was our first attempt at writing material and we had difficulty with the content and vocabulary of the work sheets. After the first term we decided to set the Third Year, because of the difficulties of dealing with such widely differing mathematical backgrounds.

During this time, the First and Second Years were taught using the text books and class lessons. We evolved the method of giving an initial period of class discussion followed by work from the textbooks, with able children working ahead at their own pace. The able children were not only given extra and harder examples — a rather futile exercise in my opinion — but they were allowed to continue to the next aspect of the topic, and when the class progressed to this work they joined in the discussion to ensure that they had completely understood the work. We found that great care had to be taken with the preparation of the class lesson, with as much use as possible being made of visual aids, such as the overhead projector and ready-made transparencies, and we found the books of published transparencies extremely useful. This method seemed to be working satisfactorily in the First Year, but in the Second Year it was not so successful. Perhaps because of their previous experiences and the content of the work, some children did not respond, and we decided to experiment further with work cards.

After discussion we decided to write work cards on: Area (including triangle and parallelogram), Relations and Coordinate Diagrams, Decimal Fractions, Fractions, Directed Numbers, Number Base and later in the term Vectors. The cards were stapled together to form a booklet on each topic and because of a paper shortage in the school we were not able to produce a booklet for each child in a Form. We were, therefore, forced to produce eight copies of each booklet for each Form, and to use all five topics at the same time. The children, as far as possible, were given a choice as to the order in which they attempted the work. This was our first experience of operating a number of different topics in the classroom at the same time. At first we were concerned over the difficulty of giving class lessons in this system, but we found after a time that they were not necessary. At first the classroom seemed to be in absolute chaos, with a number of children asking for help or reassurance at the same time. However, both we and the children soon settled into working in this way, and the children enjoyed working on their own, with some degree of freedom over the choice of topic.

This scheme still had its problems. We continued to have difficulty in writing satisfactory work cards, the work at times became too difficult too quickly, and was not practical enough; also we still had difficulty with vocabulary. Although we had our difficulties during this initial year, our experiences had shown us the difficulties and problems we had to solve to teach mixed ability groups successfully, and we had also learned much about classroom organisation to cope with an individual learning situation.

Although we had our problems setting up mixed ability teaching, we were determined to continue into the next year. We were certain that mixed ability grouping was desirable. We had been particularly pleased with the way in which children had cooperated with each other, and also because a recognisable sink group had not formed, the majority of less able children being very well motivated. However, we realised that to continue would require a tremendous amount of hard work and commitment on the part of the teachers concerned.

During the first year of the school we taught the First Year by a combination of class lessons and S M P textbooks for individual work. Although this system had worked fairly satisfactorily, we were concerned because the textbook we were using did not seem designed for individual work across the full spectrum of ability. The difficulties were not always mathematical; often reading difficulties and lack of explanation clouded the subject matter for less able children. Also, the textbook seemed to be rather inflexible, with knowledge of a chapter assumed in all subsequent chapters. Thus to start the Second Year we wanted a course which would eradicate many of the reading difficulties and inflexibilities associated with the textbook. Fortunately, about this time Cambridge University Press published S M P Cards I, and we decided to adopt this system as a basis for the work in the First Year.

The S M P Cards I cover approximately the same ground as Books A and B. The cards are supplied in three different packs, the main pack, the supplementary pack and the preliminary pack. The main pack consists of the instructional cards, the supplementary pack contains enrichment material and harder examples, and the preliminary pack contains work with basic number skills. Also required is a set of stencils for duplicating a large number of diagrams, nets and maps needed in the course.

The main pack is divided into seventeen different topics, each one frequently subdivided, to give thirty-eight sections in all. In each section there are approximately seven cards. These contain instructions and examples, and the penultimate card of each section, called the check card, revises the main points of the section, whilst the last card, called the test card, tests understanding of these points. The topics are not sequential, but there is some dependence between a few topics. For example, work on Fractions must be completed before work on Decimals can be attempted. The order of the sections in each topic and also of the cards in each section *are* sequential. Apart from ensuring that sections and cards are attempted in the correct order, children may be allowed to find their own routes through the cards.

The topic of Decimal Fractions is split into three sections. The first introduces Decimals through decimal currency, the second continues with a discussion of place value and the third deals with multiplication of Decimals by whole numbers. This is an example of a card from this topic — the second card of the second section:*

£8.30 means £8 + 30p which is £8 + 3 tenths of a pound.

Copy and complete the following:

1   £6.70 means £6 + 70p which is £... + 7 tenths of a pound.

2   £9.80 means £9 + 80p which is £9 + ... tenths of a pound.

3   £4.02 means £4 + 2p which is £4 + ... hundredths of a pound.

4   £6.07 means £6 + 7p which is £6 + ... of a pound.

5   £8.75 means £8 + 70p + 5p which is £8 + ... tenths + ... hundredths of a pound.

6   £6.23 means £6 + 20p + .p which is £. + ... + ... of a pound.

*   I am most grateful to the Cambridge University Press for permission to include this example.

You should have found that

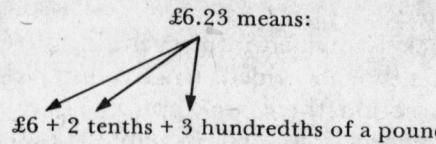

£6.23 means:

£6 + 2 tenths + 3 hundredths of a pound

In the same way

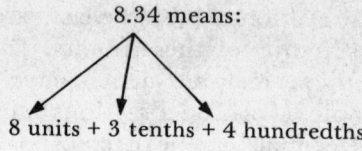

8.34 means:

8 units + 3 tenths + 4 hundredths

We can show this number on a base ten abacus with extra spikes:

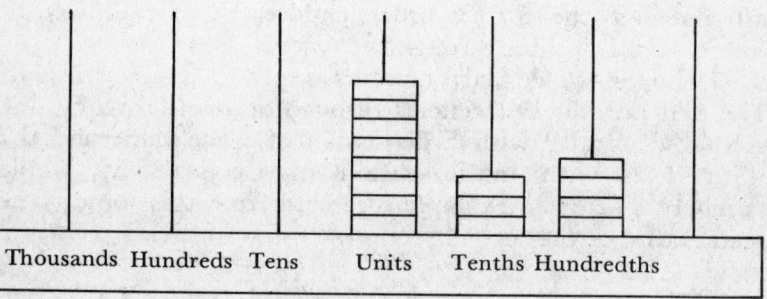

7 What label should the last spike have?

8 Draw an abacus and show the number 3491.302 on it. The layout of this card is fairly typical of the whole set and it shows the vital importance of clear and precise presentation.

For the Second Year we had no such published cards to fall back on, so we had to produce our own. First, a decision had to be taken over their format. We could produce a system of linear cards, where a child would start at the first card and work through at his own pace. This system to us seemed only slightly removed from the inflexibility of the textbooks, and would also seem to enhance feelings of inadequacy and failure in slower pupils, not able to progress as quickly as others through the cards.

Another possibility was to use the available textbooks and a system of class lessons and work sheets. This seemed to have the disadvantages firstly that the vocabulary in the textbooks would be inappropriate for part of the ability range and, secondly, that the less able children would be pressured into a false pace of work.

Finally, we decided to adopt a format similar to that explained for the SMP Cards I, although, for us, this had one enormous disadvantage — namely, that we had to have a number of different topics produced before work could start. But this method did have the advantage of allowing children to work at their own pace, with less embarrassment for less able children. Also, we thought the children would enjoy the freedom of selecting their own topics. We were fortunate to be able to obtain a single experimental set of SMP Cards II, and we used these cards as the basis of our work cards, altering, deleting and adding material. However, even with their help, we still had an enormous amount of work in the writing and duplicating of the cards. For this reason we started with the minimum number of cards, adding to them as the need arose during the year. However, in both the First and Second Years, we decided not to use the work cards for all the available lessons. Although they had many and obvious advantages, to us there seemed to be disadvantages in their exclusive use. We felt it would be wrong to discard class lessons completely, since they formed a good basis for communication, discussion and interaction between pupils. Also, we knew most subject areas would be experimenting with some type of work sheets and we were concerned that children might become bored with completely individual work in all subjects. To provide a balance we decided to use work cards for only four of our possible six lessons. The topics chosen for the other two lessons tended to be either enrichment work or topics which would gain from class discussion. Additionally, the chosen topics had to have an appeal for all abilities. We found the lessons on Sets, Statistics, Topology and Curve Stitching Patterns to be popular with all children.

Even during these class lessons, some type of work sheet was still found useful. They were often produced on the spirit duplicator and this gave us the opportunity of using different colours. Below is an example of part of a work sheet used in the Second Year after an initial class discussion on combination tables:

COPY ALL PARTS NOT IN CAPITAL LETTERS INTO
YOUR EXERCISE BOOK

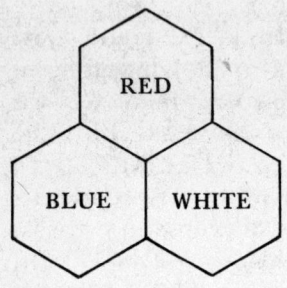

Instruction A: Leave your counter where it is.

Instruction B: Turn your counter
through 1/3 of a turn anticlock-
wise about the dot.

Instruction C: Turn your counter
through 1/3 of a turn clockwise
about the dot.

COPY AND COMPLETE THE FOLLOWING:
1   Starting on the red hexagon
    (a) after instruction B the counter is on the *blue* hexagon
    (b) after instruction C the counter is on the .... hexagon
2   Starting on the white hexagon
    (a) after instruction A the counter is on the .... hexagon
    (b) after instruction C the counter is on the .... hexagon

We can put instructions together:
e.g. starting on the blue hexagon after instruction A followed
by B, the counter is on the white hexagon.

3   Starting on the white hexagon
    (a) after instruction B followed by a repetition of this
        instruction, the counter is on the .... hexagon
    (b) after instruction C followed by B, the counter is on
        the .... hexagon

If the counter starts on the blue hexagon after instruction A
followed by B, the counter is on the white hexagon.

Which *single* instruction would take the counter from the
blue to the white hexagon?

We can say:
Instruction A followed by instruction B is the same as
instruction B.

This is shortened to:

A ⊕ B = B (⊕ means followed by)

COMPLETE THE FOLLOWING. ALWAYS START ON WHITE.

4   (a)   A ⊕ C =

    (b)   B ⊕ B =

    (c)   C ⊕ B =

The work sheet then carries on to form the combination table. Further work in this topic considered closure, identity and inverse dealing with similar non-numerical examples.

Possibly the easiest way in which I can discuss the use of both sets of work cards is to attempt to describe a typical First Year lesson, although there is so much activity during these lessons that it is impossible to set it all down here.

By the time I arrive in the classroom, children have already fetched the two boxes containing the cards and the boxes containing equipment and duplicated materials from the store-room, and some have taken their cards and have started work. My first task is to supervise the collection of materials by the remaining children, and to settle one or two noisy pupils. I then like to walk round the classroom, discussing points with individual children. I believe that as far as possible the teacher's place should be amongst the class and not sitting at the front, marking. The teacher should go to the children and not wait for them to come to him.

Walking round, I find that Mark and Michael are having difficulties with work on the equivalence of fractions, I sit down and explain, with diagrams, a few examples. I also try to show how equivalent fractions are used in addition and subtraction of fractions. Whilst I am working with this pair Jane has walked over to say that she cannot find any spotty paper. We look through the correct box and find some at the bottom.

Meanwhile, Siân walks to the front to mark an exercise. She finds she has a number of answers incorrect and so asks me for help. I discuss the work with her and I find she has not understood a particular point, so after showing her one or two examples, I direct her to re-do a particular card.

I can see across the classroom that Paul is having difficulty making his model of a dodecahendron, I move over and discuss his model. After a time he decides to undo his attempt and start again.

All this time I have been keeping an eye on Andrew who tends to be lazy and waste time. I can see he is about to start fooling around and so I talk with him for a few minutes, and try to get him interested in his work.

Matthew and Gillian are now standing at my desk waiting for test cards to be marked. After marking them I give some help over the choice of the next topic, in particular to Gillian: before choosing her topic, she wants to know what the topic Tessellations involves.

Whilst working with this pair, Heather has put up her hand for help, but by the time I can get to her, Jane has started to explain. She seems to be doing a very good job and so I leave her to continue and move to help a very weak child, who has difficulties with basic numeral skills.

Claire, a very able child, seems to be having no difficulty with the early cards on multiplication and so I direct her to miss cards and move on to the check card.

This is a very short part of a Form I lesson. I am sure it does not capture the involvement and eagerness of most of the children, and the movement and communication which they are allowed. This last point is a good one, for I feel individual learning situations lose much if the only communication the children are allowed is with the teacher. Gone are the days when children sat silently in rows listening to their teacher, although there is still a section of the profession who would judge a teacher's worth on the quietness of his class. When working with mixed ability classes, one is soon able to judge when the noise level changes from workish noise to disruptive noise.

As can be imagined, when individuals in a class are engaged on a number of different tasks, efficient classroom organisation becomes of prime importance. There are a few points worth remembering when working in a similar manner.

If possible it is better to have tables, rather than desks,

arranged in groups to accommodate six to eight children. This gives a larger surface for practical work. The children can then either be grouped according to ability, or topics studied, or allowed to sit with friends. Grouping according to ability would seem to negate most of the advantages of mixed ability classes, with the creation of a sink group. Either of the other two possibilities would be suitable. I tried grouping according to topics and found no appreciable advantages, and so I now allow the children to sit next to friends unless, of course, this is detrimental to good work.

The cards must be easily accessible and must be regularly sorted. An interested and eager child is often frustrated by searching for work cards which have been incorrectly replaced into the storage boxes. Also, stocks of duplicated material must be frequently replenished, and a careful eye kept on equipment.

There are two possible methods of storage: the cards may be placed either in the normal type of storage box with cardboard divisions separating the topics, or, as I prefer, in boxes about four or five feet long and three inches wide, divided into compartments just large enough to accommodate the cards for a particular topic. I prefer this method of storage as a larger number of children can change their cards at the same time. In Form I where the cards have been stapled into booklets, the need for easy access is not quite so acute. Since children do not have to change cards so frequently, we have stored the booklets in wallet files, one file for each section.

The old ritual of counting out rulers, protractors and other equipment is no longer possible, because throughout the lesson children are borrowing and returning equipment. The most efficient method of storage is a box with cut-outs and slots having a one-to-one correspondence with the pieces of equipment; at the end of the lesson the equipment can be checked at a glance. We store all our stationery requirements, such as squared paper, spotty paper, isometric paper and other duplicated sheets, in separate marked envelopes in a box.

The whole emphasis of this classroom organisation must be on making everything accessible to the children, so that they can equip themselves, leaving the teacher free for his main task of teaching. In any work card system it is vital for the teacher to be familiar with all the subject material, preferably by working through it, in order that he can most effectively guide and help children. This knowledge is not solely for the production of answers; with an intimate knowledge of the cards, the teacher may direct children to miss out certain cards and re-do others. However, the teacher must have a set of answers readily available, for it is amazing how quickly a queue can form while answers are worked out. Personally, I prefer to have two sets of answers. My own set contains answers and notes on all the cards; the other set is for the use of the class and does not contain answers to the test cards. I found the marking of routine work in class both tedious and time consuming, and so I wrote the answers to most of the cards on small record cards, obtainable from most stationers, and housed them in a box. The children are now free to mark their own work and only see me for marking when they have a large number of answers wrong or when they have a test card to mark.

Also of prime importance are the twin needs of assessment and efficient record keeping. The only cards to be marked and assessed by the teacher are the test cards. Attainment of these cards is graded on a scale A to E, and the effort put into the section is graded on scale 1 to 5. This twin standard of assessment is much better suited to mixed ability classes than a bare attainment mark, for often the effort put into a piece of work is as important as the level of attainment. The case of a weak child who keeps trying hard but with little success and, conversely, the case of an able child who, although, making little effort, has success, are extreme examples of the usefulness of this type of assessment. However, in my opinion, any type of grading is not as important as the verbal comment communicated to each child.

The variety of work in the classroom stresses the need for an efficient means of recording these assessments and work completed. We find it useful for both teachers and children to keep these records. The teacher is the only one to record the assessment grades, and these are written on a record sheet. This sheet contains the children's names down one side and a list of the test cards across the top. Using this, it is simple to keep a check on individual progress and records. Also, each child has his own record card. On one side of this card there is a plan of the work cards, and as each section is completed the child crosses it off the plan. On the other side the child keeps a weekly record of work completed. These cards are regularly checked to ensure that the child is making sufficient progress.

With each child at a different stage in the work cards, the setting of homework becomes difficult. I am not convinced of the importance of twice-weekly enforced homeworks in the early years of Secondary School, but pressure from the Headmaster and parents has ensured its continuation in the school, and necessitated some thought on its setting. Ideally, I would like to be able to allow children to take work cards home, so that homework is just a continuation of work started in class. Financial difficulties made the purchase of sufficient materials to operate this system impossible, as we only have just sufficient cards and the loss of any would be disastrous, but the help of a parents' typing pool might enable us to overcome this problem in the future.

In the First Year, I only occasionally set individual homeworks from the cards and then it is by instructing the class to copy down the next questions and to attempt them at home. I prefer to set a class homework after the class lesson. This is usually in the form of a project on some aspect of the work studied during the lesson and a week is allowed for the completion of the work. In the Second Year we experimented with what we called homework cards. These cards were produced for each section and contained further and harder examples, and the children were free to choose in which order the cards were attempted. This method had the advantage of revising and consolidating work previously completed, for we found a tendency for some children to forget quickly work from a particular topic. It had the disadvantage that the particular section had to be completed before the homework card could be attempted. However, this system seemed to work satisfactorily and we may experiment with it further.

Another problem we have to face is the setting of an end-of-year examination. At the end of the year the amount of work completed will vary considerably from child to child, and so the setting of a suitable paper is difficult. Also, we have the difficulty of coping with the differing abilities, either making the paper too hard or too easy for some. In our first attempt we produced a fairly long paper, instructing the children to answer as many questions as possible, with the questions getting progressively harder. This paper was not too successful as the able children were not able to answer sufficient questions to improve their scores in a marked way, and so the results were concentrated round a fairly low mean.

The next year we tried to solve this problem by setting two papers, each of an hour and each split into three sections and containing a good choice of questions. The first section consisted of short questions with answers to be written on the question paper; the second section consisted of multi-choice answer questions and the third section of harder examples involving more reasoning and answered on exercise paper. In this way we hoped to provide sufficient work for the less able to score a reasonable mark and for the more able children to show their capabilities fully. This examination was successful and gave the desired spread of marks, but extreme care must be taken in the setting of the examination if the less able are not to be put at a further disadvantage by excessive verbiage in the questions.

In general, at the moment, school examinations seem to be held for a variety of reasons — to test the retention of facts, as a spurt to revision, as practice for the future external examinations, and to satisfy parents by providing positions and percentages. In the early years of Secondary School I do not accept that all these reasons are valid, and there is in addition the difficulty of setting a meaningful examination when children have covered different work. The preferable alternative is to produce some type of continuous assessment, which should take into account not only attainment but effort. The marks obtained for classwork could form the basis of this scheme, with frequent testing, which could be carried out on an individual, group or class level, taking the place of examinations. This is a policy which must be adopted by the whole school, and for this reason, I do not think it will be possible for us to operate it in the forseeable future.

We have generally been pleased with the effects of the two work card schemes. We have been particularly impressed with the attitude of all the First Year pupils. Their involvement, eagerness and above all happiness in their tasks surpassed the natural enthusiasm that First Year children normally have for their work. However, we still have to refine our methods in order to stretch the very able to the limits of their capabilities. In the Second Year our concern has been with the other end of the ability spectrum: the less able children seemed to find difficulty in parts of the course in following the development of a topic through the individual cards. Some also found difficulty in persevering with harder topics, preferring to try to drop the topic and start something new, without the teacher's knowledge.

In future in the First Year we hope to make far more use of the opportunities for omitting cards, leaving the very able more time to tackle the enrichment and harder work. We also hope to be able to produce more supplementary material, not only for the able, but containing some open-ended problems for the whole class.

In the Second Year we are restructuring our work card scheme to try to give more help to the weaker children, whilst making the work more open-ended. Rather than having a large number of topics operating simultaneously, we have broken down the course into approximately eight units, each unit will consist of two, three or four topics, depending upon their length. These topics will be written on work cards similar to the ones we previously produced, and they will form a common core of work which we will expect all children to attempt. In addition, we are producing supplementary cards containing further work on the topics, enrichment work and open-ended problems. We do not expect children to attempt all the available work from this section, but rather to choose a point of particular interest to them and develop it as far as possible. We hope, in this way, to make Mathematics far more open-ended, but still keeping a certain common core of work. One unit is going to consist of the basic work on multiplication and division of Fractions, Tessellations and Area; further work will include invest-igations into areas on pinboards, growth of side to area of squares, tangrams, why some figures tessellate, and Pythag-oras' Rule.

We shall have pairs of Forms working on the same unit, with sufficient numbers of topic booklets for each child to be issued with, so easing the problem of setting homework. Individual teachers will be able to use the available materials as they wish, but we hope to incorporate a class lesson at the beginning of each topic. In this lesson, using class discussion, we will endeavour to trace the development of the topic as it appears on the work cards and we shall also try to indicate some possible further lines of enquiry. The children will then work through the cards, and subsequently progress to the supplementary work. At a suitable time the next topic will be introduced. We will specify a certain time, hopefully suf-ficient for all, for the completion of the unit, when all the common core work has to be completed. In this way we hope to give a target for the less well motivated, whilst retaining some of the possibilities for selection of work and allowing for different levels of enquiry in the supplementary work.

Perhaps some teachers will wonder, as I did, at first, how we can have an open-ended situation in Mathematics. In my opinion this can happen in two ways. First, by allowing a child to investigate a topic as far as he wishes or to the limit of his ability. For example, a child working on Pascal's triangle and Fibonacci's sequence could investigate the life and work of the mathematicians Blaise Pascal and Leonardo de Pisa (nicknamed Fibonacci), or look at the connection between Pascal's triangle and probability, or Fibonacci's sequence and architecture, or the internal structures of the two number patterns; in fact, there are many possible lines of enquiry. Obviously, for this to be a success a large number of different books must be available, and so a large Mathematics library is essential.

Secondly, there is the type of open-ended situation where the children are invited to investigate a particular problem and arrive at their own conclusions. A fairly typical example of this line is:

Fermat proved that certain prime numbers are the sum of two square numbers. For example

$$5 = 2^2 + 1^2$$
$$29 = 5^2 + 2^2$$

For each of the prime numbers less than 100 find out whether or not it can be written as the sum of two square numbers. Can you find out anything about the prime numbers which are the sum of two squares?

This example has been taken from a very interesting and useful book by C. S. Banwell, K. D. Saunders and D. G. Tahta, called *Starting Points*, published by Oxford University Press, which contains many other similar examples and interesting problems. Further open-ended problems can be found in *Fifteen Starters for the Secondary Classroom*, published by the Association of Teachers of Mathematics.

Our experiences have convinced us that mixed ability teaching is good, although I think all of us would agree to it being very much harder work than a streamed situation. We have been forced to examine our aims and subjects in the early secondary years, and we have also involved ourselves in the writing of materials, which, I am sure, would not previously have happened. The gearing of teaching methods to the individual child has made us more aware of children as individuals and not just as a member of an 'O' Level, or CSE or unexaminable set. Through the involvement of the teacher with small groups or individuals, teaching has become more intimate, rather than the impersonal situation of a class lesson. We are now far more concerned with the individual mathematical development of children, rather than the assimilation of a set amount of Mathematics during a specified period. When we set for Mathematics in the Third Year, we now find difficulty in recognising the set as a homogeneous group. We are more aware of the spread of ability, and many of the techniques developed primarily for mixed ability groups are very useful with these sets. We now frequently produce assignment sheets which, together with the textbooks, allow children to work at their own pace through a topic.

As I have said earlier, we are very pleasd with the attitudes of the children towards the subject. Most children are enthusiastic and interested in their work. We have very few discipline problems, perhaps because the children are interested, perhaps because of the degree of organisation and preparation for lessons, or because we have not created a sink group with all its attendant problems. We are satisfied with the standard of learning in the subject. The weaker children have most certainly benefited, for they now have confidence and interest in the subjects, and the able have not been sacrificed, for they have been allowed to work at their own pace and not one artificially imposed by the teacher.

We realise that our system for handling mixed ability groups has its shortcomings, but this is not a definitive statement on mixed ability teaching. Rather it is an effort to explain how courses and methods have evolved in a mixed ability situation which we consider to be right and to show that there are no instant answers. The transference of concentration from the class to the individual involves a total re-appraisal of methodology: evaluation and adjustment must be made continuously.

6 Science
David Bosworth

This description of the setting up of an individualised scheme of work for the Sciences is presented in the hope that it will give some ideas to teachers who want to start similar schemes or who are faced with the possibility of teaching mixed ability groups. The scheme set up was one which suited the personalities of the teachers involved in the pilot project so it is unlikely that others will wish to accept it *in toto*. The reasons for following a particular course of action are given so that the reader may decide for himself which course of action he wishes to follow. At the time this course of action suited the conditions as they appeared. Needless to say alterations in the conditions would lead to different approaches, but within the same framework of an individualised scheme.

The need for an individualised work programme was inherent in the original specification for the Kibworth Science Project. This objective did not spring from the need or desire to teach in mixed ability groups but from the subject itself. When deciding the aims of a subject the first consideration must concern the choice between child and subject. Are we to consider the amount of material which the child is going to know at the end of the course or are we going to consider the behaviour of the child as a result of the course to which we subject him. Behaviour, in this sense, to mean the total child as he develops into adulthood; his attitudes, interests and ways in which he deals with his fellows. If the consideration is only the amount of knowledge absorbed, then there is no problem other than knowing what material he ought to know. For a teacher who is only going to think along these lines, the set syllabus of an external examination saves the bother of having to think too much. It provides not only his justification for the subject but also the necessary reason for teaching any topic which happens to be there. As soon as the effects of any particular piece of material on the general development of the child are brought into the arguments, however, it ceases to be quite so simple. Can, for instance, the teaching of heredity be justified by the additional claim that it will train the child in racial tolerance? This particular claim may well rely on the teaching method, and the attitudes of the teacher far more than on the subject material itself. We will return to this point later.

The aim most often claimed for the teaching of Science is that of training in Scientific Method. As it stands it is, as a teaching aim, of very little value. It becomes necessary to define much more precisely what is meant by Scientific Method. One must then show how this particular aim can be accomplished. Generally, in using the term Scientific Method, teachers mean a particular way in which a problem should be solved. Having been presented with a problem, one will solve it by a process which involves the setting up of a hypothesis, testing it by experimentation and, should it be found necessary, amending the hypothesis. The process may be repeated on the amended hypothesis. For the research scientist the process may also include the isolation of the problem. In school the teacher may find this a necessary part of his job or of the child's work. If the aim is to teach ordinary people to deal with problems which occur in their everyday life by testing the possible answers, there seems little to be gained in asking them to isolate the problem in the first place. Even then, however, the problem of transfer arises. There is little direct evidence to suggest that a scientist will apply the testing routine to everyday problems. Unless the transfer of Scientific Method to everyday experience is explicitly expressed, little transfer is likely to occur. This would entail the growth of the syllabus to include material which was not directly Science orientated, but which could be dealt with in the Scientific manner. The value of teaching Scientific Method will, for the majority of pupils, be confined to an understanding of the way in which the scientist works. In this it will have solved a little of the problem of understanding the attitudes of scientists as compared with those of others. It is hardly the justification for a particular method of teaching which is going to continue for three or more years. At the same time, the teaching of Scientific Method does not indicate any particular syllabus. The actual material taught can be anything, as long as it is dealt with in this particular way.

Closely related to the first aim is that of getting the pupils to draw inferences from data. It differs from the testing of a hypothesis in that it may only deal with testing and not the setting up of the hypothesis in the first place. In general such an aim leads to the setting up of a great deal of practical work from which data is collected and conclusions are drawn. This sort of work has been a part of science teaching for many years and the contemporary movement is towards more experimental work — child centred or in the form of demonstration by the teacher. In many ways this is the same as the idea presented in the aim of teaching Scientific Method. In so many cases the statement of aims is designed in such a way that it determines the teaching method rather than the material to be considered. Indeed, most of the books putting forward the aims are doing so in justification of the particular material which they contain.

Another way of looking at the problem of how and what to teach can be that of starting with the child. In considering the child we can assess what we have and how we wish to change this in the teaching which is going to take place. The aims of the course may well be the same as those of other subjects when the decision is taken in this way. There are two ways of looking at this way of presenting the child with a Science syllabus. The child already has certain interests which can be used in the course; the course can, therefore, be designed to work with the child's individual interests. The second method becomes rather more complicated since it needs to look at the growth of the child, at his capabilities and the way in which he, personally, is developing and will develop. Unless the teacher is going to take those topics which are said to be of interest to all children of a certain age group, both these starting-points require an individual approach. Both these approaches also make the particular topics which are going to be included in the syllabus secondary to the interests and development of the child.

A teaching method which stresses the importance of the interests of the child may be criticised on the basis that it ignores the major concepts in Science which the child ought to know. A dichotomy can arise — those who stress the importance of the way in which the child works against those who stress the material which the child will learn. This leads to an argument about the importance of facts, with one side saying that the factual content of the syllabus is of no importance. The other side maintains that certain facts are of value since they will be needed for some reason or other — for follow-up work or for a proper understanding of the present work. However, the argument can become a pseudo-dichotomy, in which it appears that one side is arguing that the children *never* need or obtain any facts. This extreme position is contrasted with the other methods as if the facts were the only thing which was being presented and no thought was being given to the way in which the child obtained these facts. It becomes clear that both sides are being driven into extreme positions in defence of a particular teaching method. Whatever methods are used, the child is bound to obtain some information. Whether this information is of value to the child or considered to be valuable by the observer is another point altogether.

My aim here is to present a scheme which has been built up in an empirical way. Ideas were tried out and amended as they were seen to be deficient in the particular situation in which they were tested.

The first step in individualising the course was to present the children with the material which would be used to answer a problem. As they completed this one piece of work it was checked by the teacher who then carried the learning on to the next stage. This normally entailed the theory behind the experiment — why this particular result might have been expected to have occurred and how the results might be given a more general form than that presented from one experiment alone. The problem which was encountered by this method of presenting the work was that there were too many children wanting information at the same time. This would not have been too great a problem if the information required had been the same for all of the children, or even for many of them. It was amazing the number of *different* problems which were encountered from the same piece of experimental work.

Once the decision had been made to make the work as individual as possible, the growth of the scheme proceeded with changes being made when it became necessary, either so that the children would gain as much as possible from the work presented or to deal with organisational problems. Once the scheme was individualised there were more problems, probably, than had been found in the class-teaching situation. The difference, now, was that the precise nature of the problem could be ascertained and we felt, too, that we could deal with the difficulties, instead of having to say, 'This is the system, there is nothing I can do about it.'

The next progression was to add programmes to the scheme. The purpose of the programme was to give the child the basic 'follow-up' material required. Programmes were written which gave the child the problem, suggested a way of solving it with an experiment and then (after the experiment had been checked by the teacher) went on to deal with the generalisations which could be made as a result of the discovery. In this way the scheme might be said to be one of controlled heuristics. The children were finding things out for themselves, but the order of presentation was decided by the teacher. Within the scheme as we worked it there was a need to make sure that the child arrived at the normally accepted conclusion to the experiment. The programme proceeded on this assumption. It was, therefore, necessary for the teacher to check the work which the child had done in the laboratory before he went on from the experiment. This checking can be done in a variety of ways. In this scheme the teachers were agreed that, wherever possible, the children should not be told 'This is wrong, you should have seen this and so concluded that.' The methods used were, first, to accept all results as they stood and if the conclusion agreed with the results but did not answer the problem which was set, suggest that an attempt be made to do this. The child could repeat the experiment or adapt it to give a better answer. Secondly we faced the problem of the wrong conclusion from the results which the child had. This would lead to discussion of the results leading onto the child seeing, for himself, the error of his thinking so that he can put the conclusion right. It would not be the policy of the teachers involved in the scheme to give the child the right answer. Similarly, other 'mistakes' which the child made could be cleared up with a pupil—teacher discussion. Such discussions would normally be in the ratio of 1:1 but other children could be included if they had the same difficulties at the same time. It would also be possible to put together children who would profit by discussion of a topic between themselves. This might be done to see if an explanation given to one child had been of any value to him. Could he explain the material to another child?

Another point at which discussion could take place, when the programme instructed the child to check with the teacher, was at the end of each section of work. The child would complete a test as he finished each part of the programme. This test would tell the teacher how effective the programme had been and where the child had not understood the work presented. Such tests could lead to corrections of the programme but they also ensured that the child was in full possession of the facts raised before going on to another piece of work. The rest formed a summary of the work covered by the programme and, with the experimental work, would be the material that the child had available for revision. While the particular school in which the scheme was set up did not have any examinations in the first three years subsequent programmes in the Science series did refer the child to information contained in the earlier work.

From what has been said, it is obviously of great importance what sort of programmes are used in the scheme. A few published programmes were used in our scheme for comparison purposes, but the majority of the material was written for use in the school. This was necessary, largely due to the lack of material which incorporated experimental work. Some programmes which are now becoming available do include experiments, but at the time when this scheme was started there was none available.

In the case of this scheme the programmes were intended to link work which would give the children material towards G C E. The first thing, which happened in the writing of programmes, for this reason, was a discussion about the actual material which was going to be included in the programme. The next stage was to decide where the work would be best undertaken. This was so that the children could make use of the lab. facilities where they were available, rather than moving material to the children. The scheme was also built up round specialist teachers so that each teacher took on responsibility for his own particular main interest.

Having decided where the work would be undertaken (and which teacher would be responsible for it), the writing of the frames was done by each of the teachers. By consultation at this stage it can be ensured that the work does link up across the sciences. A coordinated scheme of work is achieved.

Much has been written about the frame size in programmes. The size of the frame — indeed all corrections on the materials we used — was decided on the basis of empirical evidence. What worked in the actual class situation was continued into the other programmes in preparation. As with most programme writers we started by writing programmes with too much information in each frame. This was gradually cut down until the optimum level for maximum success was reached. The final frame size became much larger than that normally advocated. It was found that, as long as the child had to answer questions through the frame, it would be satisfactory. Later programmes, for example, have lengthened to quarto sheet size with something for active involvement by the child throughout the length of the frame. Illustrated frames had better chance of success than straight reading material. In fact the use of strip cartoon not only increased the amount of interest in the frame but also helped in the learning which took place.

Originally the syllabus paper as the basis for the factual material was that of the traditional 'O' Levels in Physics, Chemistry or Biology. Since the aims of the scheme were concerned with the student's ability to carry out processes and handle data the cognitive content is not important. The fact that *every* child carried out his own work, used his own data to complete *all* sections which he undertook was considered to be more important than the actual factual material presented. Such a course as that described here could, in fact, form the basis for a C S E or G C E Mode Three Science qualification. The idea of measuring a student's abilities in the processes rather than by the pure remembering of Science is not entirely new and would provide a more useful assessment than the present forms of measurement.

When such a scheme of individualised work is set up the requirements of both lab. space and equipment change. This scheme was deliberately arranged so that the equipment which was available could still be used and so that any extra materials required would only be those which any lab. might expect to have. Despite the fact that every child is now doing every experiment there is no need to increase the basic equipment. While they are doing all the experiments themselves they are not doing so at the same time. The work has been arranged with several 'starting-points' so that the child follows the work through in a different order from his colleagues. It is also possible, of course, to arrange the order and type of work to suit the abilities of the child. What used to be demonstration experiments are now done by the children. This not only makes better use of the equipment but has been shown to give the child a better understanding of what he is trying to find out in the experiment. Additional materials are needed when dealing with the less able child and, for the brighter ones, more enrichment material is needed.

As far as the less able child is concerned it is, first and foremost, of paramount importance not to underestimate him or to be guided too much by his own estimation of himself. The first thing we tell all children, as a group, is that they should inform a teacher if they are unable to read. Since all the usual material presented in the scheme is written this is a *very* necessary prerequisite for the course. Reading ages are also sent on from the Junior School and these are checked for children with very low reading ability. Since the scheme is an individual one, however, more time can be spent in finding out the exact position of the individual child instead of giving a blanket 'non-reading' stamp on a group which happens to be the lowest stream.

In all but the very worst cases the child is likely to be given a simple programme on which to start. It is made clear at this time that he should ask whenever in difficulties and these children are carefully checked to see how they are progressing. If reading still presents a problem then other forms of work are arranged.

Having decided that the child is not capable of working the normal programmes he is usually put onto tape-recordings. These tapes cover the same work as the programmes but the material can now be presented orally. The child will still carry out his own experiments in the same way as everyone else and he will write them up. The writing up calls for careful marking by the teacher. In the case of a child who has difficulty in reading and writing the material, while perfectly all right from the point of view of results and conclusions, may be badly presented. This is also true of the brighter child and the teacher is again put in the position where he has to use his discretion. It is possible for him to say that the work of one child is well done and of another that he could do better.

It might be thought that this sort of discrimination by the teacher would cause children, all in the same group, to complain. This is not the case. The attitude to each other in a mixed ability group is not quite the same as it is in streamed situations. This is probably due, in the main, to the way in which the groups are organised. A streamed group is generally a highly competitive one and any work done is going to affect the child's chance of coming out top of the class. Obviously work which is manifestly inferior should not receive higher marks and the children know this. In a mixed ability group there is no competition to get to the top, so the same sorts of pressures to value each other's work do not occur.

Another method of giving work to the less able child is to present, also on tape if it is found necessary, material which might be said to have a greater bearing on the daily life of the child. This is also an aim which can be said to apply to all children so material which is, primarily, prepared for less able children becomes available to the whole group. Part of the reason why this becomes a possibility is that the material which is presented is not only on tape. Included with the taped material are slides (viewed through individual viewers) and, where it is appropriate, by written material. For the non-reader this helps the aural and visual link, which could lead to an improvement in his reading ability. Indeed, it has been discovered within our scheme that children who are not considered to be readers and are given extra reading lessons can cope with the Science work given to them in a most satisfactory manner. They often take longer than the better readers to complete the work. Complete it they do and obtain very satisfactory marks on the final test. If only we are able to persuade these children to get through the initial work the self-confidence engendered through the pleasure in completing something well increases the possibility of the child making further progress.

As a consequence of this procedure the work of the less able children has been made less formal. At the same time much of the material initially prepared for less able children has been incorporated into the general scheme of work. This has led to the alteration of the course from being a purely 'O' Level entrance. The work is much more geared to a general scientific understanding than can be obtained by a slavish following of the usual 'O' Level Science courses.

One way often used to help the less able, a way which is not frequently put into practice within this scheme, is to put them with someone else. This is the normal group practice but had not been followed very closely in this scheme since it was conceived as an individual scheme. If ways can be produced to help these children to do their own work (and work which they are pleased to call *their own*) then this has seemed well worth while. However, there are children who respond better when with another child. There are children, particularly some of the girls, who are only too pleased to have someone to look after. These sorts of groups tend to form themselves so a close watch has to be kept by the teacher to make sure that they are satisfactory groups. If a child is seen to be relying entirely on someone else, then efforts are made to get this child to do at least some of the work for himself. The scheme became a part individual and — where it was needed — a part collaborative structure.

When dealt with in this way it becomes noticeable that there are less children who cannot do the work than seems to be the case with streamed classes and examination syllabi. In a year of 135 children only 14 were found to be incapable of following a normal course of work which had, as its aim, some form of academic advancement. These 14 children were not wasting their time or doing no work of any value. They were put to other work which was designed to have a definite outcome. It should also be mentioned that they were not always children who had low measured I Q's or reading ages. Their success problem was something else.

The whole point in changing the scheme of teaching has been to lead the greatest number of children to the highest level of success of which thy are capable.

The bright child is not neglected within such a scheme. It has often been said, so often that it takes on the ring of truth, that the bright child will succeed despite his teachers. On the other hand, it has been shown that some children are not doing as well as they might in the ordinary school and so are taken out for special tuition. This has led to the setting up of schools for the exceptional child, where he often ends up with the pupil to teacher ratio better than in the ordinary school and his exceptional ability is brought to the fore. Consequently there must be children who do not succeed but who could succeed, if the conditions in which they are working are suitable. In fact, there can be children who have been classed quite low, probably called a nuisance because of their behaviour, in the normal school.

Can an individualised scheme of work do anything more than the ordinary school for these exceptional pupils or for those pupils who are slightly lower down the ability scale? Results within the scheme would seem to suggest that it is possible. Basically a programmed course allows, because of the programme, all children to gain good marks on a final test. It gives everyone the chance of achieving high academic results on the work which is done. At the same time the better worker can cover more ground – can complete more programmes than do the others. In practice the children who cover the most number of programmes also obtain the highest marks in final tests. This need not be the case. A fast

worker may be fast to the detriment of his understanding.
The really able child, therefore, stands out as both a fast and
accurate worker. Some children in such a scheme as this are
going to complete a full syllabus in far shorter time than their
contemporaries or, for that matter, would be the case if they
had to work to the rate decided by the teacher as the
optimum for the group in front of him.

Besides being able to work through the whole course in a
shorter time there is another method of dealing with the fast
worker. This is the form taken by the Nuffield projects in
which there is a basic minimum which every child is expected
to cover. Over this there are extra experiments which can be
done if there is time. Many teachers give these extra
experiments to the faster workers. This is necessary when the
next piece of work must start off with all the children at the
same point and, in some cases, is claimed to be the best
system. There is a decision to be made between finishing the
whole course in as short a time as possible or giving the
brightest children more practice on each topic. Since the
programmes used in this scheme are designed to give the
average child as much practice as is required for a full
understanding of the topic under discussion it seems unlikely
that the bright child is going to need more practice. It seems
much better to give him the next piece of work or to give
him something which is going to take the topic further.

Besides additional experiments on the same topic greater
concern can be placed on the application of facts discovered
to everyday problems. Also used in this scheme were extra
reading assignments using magazine materials which the lab.
had available. Second Year children who were completing
their work well were given magazine articles to look at. After
the first session with these they might well come back saying
that they could not understand it. This will lead to a
discussion of the first part of the article: Can we rephrase this
to make more sense to you? What about checking the
experiment? Does this link up with what you have learned so
far? And so on. The child then has another look at the
material and, in most cases, ends up with an idea at least of
what it was all about and a request to take the book home
for a longer period to have a look at more of it.

Because the scheme is individualised, it gives the teacher more chance to lead each individual to his optimum level of conceptual achievement. At the same time individuals can be taken off work which proves to be beyond their capabilities without making it obvious to the whole of the class that these children are failures. Even failure on one piece of work, which is broadcast to the world, can be sufficient to label the child in the eyes of himself and of his contemporaries, a complete failure when nothing could be further from the truth.

The child who is a nuisance in class because he is 'under-employed' is no problem to deal with. He can very easily be given work which is in keeping with his own capabilities. He can be given work which will be more likely to appeal to him than the work which he had been doing in the past since this had obviously been unsuitable. The real problem in this case, however, is not what work to give to the able child but to distinguish him from the other children who are behaviour problems. A child who is given work which is too hard for him will often behave in the same way as the child who is given work which is too easy for him. The teacher must distinguish between these children and give them work accordingly. Often this can only be done by a trial and error approach. However, this need not be as bad as it sounds since the teacher can invite the cooperation of the child in finding the work which is most suitable. Such an approach can well persuade the child that the teacher is trying to do his best to help, and lead to greater cooperation between the two when other decisions have to be made.

It can be claimed that the bright child does not suffer from contact with his less well endowed contemporaries as long as the work which will lead him to full cognitive development is available. Indeed, under an individualised scheme there seems to be a far better chance for more children to achieve academic excellence than would be the case if they were streamed into groups which were supposed to progress at the same rate. In the same way it is more likely that children covering an individualised course up to sixteen will be usefully employing their capabilities at all stages. If the work becomes too difficult they can easily be switched to other

more interesting material as they see it. At the same time it
would seem reasonable to suggest that this work could form
part of a Mode Three examination presentation. That the
work appears interesting to the student does not mean that it
is not suitable for examination purposes.

It has generally been held that children need to be shown
scientific phenomena and then have them explained. This has
been put into practice in the demonstration lesson followed
by a class 'discussion' of the results, but a new trend has been
finding its way into the thinking of some teachers. As part of
this new trend has been the idea that what the child has seen
for himself and manipulated for himself he would come to
understand. This thinking has been supported by examples
such as the way in which adults will come to terms with a
new situation forgetting that adults who are capable of
coming to terms with a new situation have a wider cognitive
background on which to draw. It also ignores the fact that
there are adults who need a great deal of help in coming to
terms and others who, despite lavish amounts of help, do not
come to terms with new situations. These are not 'special'
cases but normal adult peoples.

As part of the trials with the situation which we were
building up some children were given the opportunity of
finding things out for themselves. These were, usually, those
children whom we considered to be somewhat above the
normal and they were given experimental situations in which
they might well learn something for themselves. It was found
that a certain amount of help (in some cases, a great deal of
help) had to be given before the child could be said to have
understood the work he was doing. At the secondary stage of
education it was considered that the child should be able to
understand the main linking concepts which would help to
explain new situations when they arose. In other words our
definition of *understand* comes to mean that the child will so
internalise the information which he has gathered that he will
be able to make use of it. As a step in this direction the child
would be able to verbalise his findings. Where appropriate he
would be able to link previous findings with those which he
now discovered in an experimental situation.

In giving the child only the experiment and expecting

some carry over to a wider field of thought and application we discovered that we were expecting too much. In some cases the amount of guidance which was necessary was small but there were indications that the child needed to be taught how to use the information which he had received. That he could more easily make use of the information which he had found out for himself was not in doubt. A combination of past experience, personal manipulation of the materials and guidance in how to apply the new material was found to be the most useful for complete understanding.

It should be noted that the idea of giving the child the right answer is not what is proposed. From the child's personal experience the teacher must guide him towards a fuller understanding. This is why certain procedures were adopted in this scheme. The child is not *given* the answer to a question, nor is he told that an experiment is wrong. The purpose of the programmes is to guide the child towards a full understanding of the facts raised in the experiment. Where 'mistakes' in understanding or in experimental work are made the teacher's rôle is that of guide. By the use of questioning the pupil can be led to see what has gone on. It should be noted that the questioning that results from experimental work may well be to get the child to see that he has not, in fact, answered the problem which was set but some other problem. Then the questioning continues to find a way in which the actual problem can be answered. Where a child has brought the complaint, 'I can't get this right', such questioning can end with the teacher saying 'See, you knew it all along really.' This has been found to be very satisfactory from the child's point of view in that he is likely to say, 'Ah, yes I see now' and leave happy. Another adult watching such a discussion is likely to say that the teacher has given the child the answer. In some respects this may be so but it *does not appear this way to the child* who has had to think his way through the discussion.

Consequently it would be a natural extension of our courses to say that many children will progress while gradually making less demands on the teacher. The need to undertake explanations will diminish as the cognitive background on which the child can call gradually increases. Older children, or those whose understanding is increased at any age, can continue with a rather less structured background approach than that needed in the early stages.

What an individualised scheme of work does allow is a certain amount of free work. Since the teacher is still in charge of the situation it is his decision as to when and how this might be incorporated. If all the children in a lab. are doing work of their own choosing then the situation can become difficult from an administrative point of view. That the Primary School teacher can apparently do this is due to the different situation in which he is placed. There need not be such a need for theory and for the generalisations which are going to be required at the later stage and he is not dealing with all his class doing experimental work at the same time. Indeed, he is likely to be dealing with less children altogether. Since the work being dealt with will be at a lower level of academic achievement there is less likely to be the question 'Has the child done work, or gained some understanding of, the material which will help to make this topic he has chosen meaningful?'

The general organisation that developed from the beliefs and ideals embodied in a programmed, individualised approach was also affected by the physical constraints of the school. It was envisaged that a team teaching approach should be adopted for a combined science course where a 'specialist teacher' would be responsible for particular sections of the work. The syllabus which was to be covered was agreed by the team of teachers involved and was, basically, a standard science scheme of work. At a later date elements of the Nuffield science projects were added to update the scheme and any material considered to be of sufficient interest was made available. Each of the teachers concerned agreed to be responsible for particular sectors of the work, linked to their own interests and expertise. While a child was working through that part he would come under the tuition of the teacher responsible for writing the section and his work during that period of time would be checked by him.

At the beginning of the First Year children are randomly assigned to a group linked to a teacher for the first few

lessons or series of lessons which are arranged to introduce
pupils to the layout of labs and certain basic procedures. At
this time everyone is taught to use a bunsen and to recognise
metric measurements. Groups with Biology teachers are,
while the weather is still likely to be fine, given a survey of
the local environment on which much of their future lessons
would be dependent. At this stage groups are alternated so
that all the children obtain this basic training which, if
necessary, can be varied to include other material seen to be
of value. At the end of this section the children are given
their first assignments by the teachers with whom they
happen to be. Each subject area has several 'starting-points'
so that facilities at this stage are not overloaded. At the end
of the first assignment the child moves onto the next. This
will, generally, be related to the first and form part of a
sequence of material taking him from one teacher to another.
Different children will, after the initial week or so, be moving
between the teachers within the team following a sequence of
material judged to be suitable for them.

The fact that children need to move from teacher to
teacher (or, for that matter, from topic to topic) individually
calls for careful record keeping. In the Kibworth Science
Project each child has a record card which contains information about the work he is doing. Attempts were made to
include an objective assessment of his progress alongside the
date of starting and completion and the final test score
achieved. An attempt was made, on the record cards, to give
an assessment of the actual amount of work done entirely on
his own. Where a great deal of help was required this was
stated on the card. No attempt was made to grade this as
good or bad since it was merely a statement of what had been
done with a particular piece of work.

As the child moved from teacher to teacher, so his record
card passed on. If a teacher has a record card in his possession
he is responsible for the work of the child at that time. While
he will normally ensure that a sequence of work is carried out
in his lab. area he can, if he so wishes, or if he sees the need
for it, change the work pattern to suit the requirements of
the child. Once the children have embarked on their
individual work it is unlikely that they will be brought

together for a class lesson. Indeed many of them resented being taken away from their own work when this was tried out on a regular basis. Reasons given for including class work generally cited discussions as being all important. Within the context of the Kibworth Science Project we considered that this was not really relevant.

The suggestion that children carried out discussion in class lessons where there was an interchange of ideas seemed, on the basis of past experience, to be somewhat exaggerated. Science class lessons were either another excuse for the teacher to expound or they were pseudo-discussion in which the teacher did his best to persuade the children that they were designing the work. This, of course, will vary from teacher to teacher and from class to class, but the individual discussion carried out in our scheme did seem to cover the chance of real discussion with an adult mind which could be more stimulating than child to child discussion. It also lessened the defects of full class lessons. If the need arose or if it were considered to be of use the children can be brought into discussion between themselves. This is often arranged between both high and low levels of ability as well as between children of the same ability.

Also possible within the programmed scheme are child discussions without any teacher involvement. These are not always on the topics being studied but, perhaps surprisingly, often are. Teacher to pupil discussions may not always be on Science. One of the advantages of the individualisation of a scheme of work is the fact that the teacher can come to know the children better. Spontaneous discussions can take place and, even those which do not directly concern Science, can be made use of in the learning situation. It would seem that the discussion possible in an individualised situation would give more scope than was possible in a class situation without the drawbacks. The main drawback to any class lesson is the involvement of *all* children. The most obviously left out are the timid children. In many cases they have something to add to the discussion, often they have thought of something which has completely passed the others by but are frightened to speak up. It was partly for these children that the scheme was started and in it they can be persuaded to put their ideas forward to the teacher or to other children.

Two other, similar, reasons given for wanting class lessons are that new stimulation can be given for the next work to be done and to keep the course progressing at a reasonable rate. The first of these, the presentation lessons, does not apply in the situation which we have built up. The value of this lesson is to present ideas on one topic so that the children can follow-up the part or parts which appeal to them. Obviously such lessons are suited to a scheme which has the children working on the same topic at the same time and, at some point, it has to be decided that the topic has gone on long enough. A new topic will be introduced. In the scheme here it was decided that this was not satisfactory and each child should be given the time required to finish the work which he was given. Presentation lessons would not be required to start off any particular piece of work. Similarly, it was felt that the work could be kept going at a reasonable rate by making sure that each child was working at his optimum speed through the programmes.

Class lessons could be made of use in an individualised scheme if it were found necessary to deal with mistakes which were always cropping up or to instil some eagerness on the part of the children. With the scheme used and the teachers who were taking part in it this was not found to be necessary. The sorts of errors which did crop up were slightly different for each child unless there was some obvious deficiency in the programme. Such faults as these were eradicated by rewriting. The biggest problem was in the writing up of experiments or of doing essay-type answers in tests. In both cases it was still felt that the best way of dealing with the problem was in an individual way. In this way there was no pressure on all the children to write up experiments in the same way. This is of vital importance if the child, particularly the less able child, is to be given a chance to do work which is in keeping with his or her ability.

As has already been said, the children are now carrying out those experiments which used to be demonstrations. This means that class demonstrations are no longer required and the consideration has only to be 'can the children safely carry out the experiment on their own?' For the most part they can, but it was decided to omit from the course the controversial preparation of oxygen. Less explosive methods than the heating of a chlorate mixture were tried but found to be unsatisfactory so the children do not prepare oxygen. They do test it using gas from a cylinder installed in the lab., collecting a gas jar full as they require it. In this case the method of collection was retained as the displacement of water so that the children had experience of this. Other difficult and dangerous experiments could not be circumscribed so easily. They were a major part of the work being presented and without them there would be a loss in the final understanding of the child. In these cases other methods of presentation were tried out. In some instances the experiment was set up permanently so that, when it was required, the teacher had only to run through it. This sort of arrangement was satisfactory for very short experiments but for material which took longer films, illustrated descriptions and the like were used.

It could be said that illustrations were a poor substitute for good demonstrations. This could well be true but the number of good demonstrations is in question and, since these form only a small part of the whole course, the child is missing very little. In fact, from the child's point of view, it is better to be reading about something, in an interesting way, than to be taken from his work to watch what the teacher decided to do. The number of experiments which it was considered were beyond the child were very small. Once given the chance of doing the work himself it was surprising how much the child was able to do with some benefit to himself. It became clear that, in the past, we had seriously underestimated the capabilities of the children. Indeed, I have heard Sixth Form teachers saying, quite seriously, that their children would not be able to handle material which was on show *for the early years in the Nuffield scheme*. They have shown in this project that some children are capable of handling quite complex materials and situations, in a completely individualised situation, without interference during the work, we have shown that most children are capable of sophisticated work.

Breakage is always a problem when children are given access to large quantities of apparatus. This has not proved a very serious problem in the scheme, where the breakage rate has fallen over that found in group experiment situations. The reason for this is partly due to the fact that the work is seen to be the child's and his responsibility, partly to the fact that the lab. is not overcrowded with children doing experiments at the same time, and partly to the fact that there is no time limit on the completion of the work. When the children know that they are able to work through to a satisfactory conclusion, whatever happens, there is no rush and less chance of breakage or other accidents.

III THE UNSTREAMED SCHOOL

7 Preparing for De-streaming

A few years ago the members of a study group in which I was involved were reduced to tears of mirth as a colleague described how the school where he worked had launched — and abandoned — its mixed ability experiment. A school of the type favoured for the attentions of the arch-critics of comprehensivisation — working on split sites — it was formed by the amalgamation of a mixed Grammar School and two single-sex Secondary Modern Schools, all the buildings of which continued to be used in the new combine. The Headmaster decided that certain educational ideas he held should be implemented in the school early in its development, when the staff were anticipating change and had not geared their work to a gradually evolved pattern. Late in the summer term of the first session — when teachers from the hitherto three separate schools were still eyeing each other warily and when problems consequent upon the physical scattering of the school's buildings were still unresolved — the Head pronounced that when the new term opened two afternoons per week would be devoted to a full year-group working on an Inter-Disciplinary Enquiry basis, whilst all the First Year forms would be organised in mixed ability groups! The story is not apocryphal, though, inevitably, it was embellished in the retelling, and its conclusion can easily be forecast. By the end of the following half-term, the staff's lack of understanding and knowledge of the reasons for change, together with their lack of preparation, involvement and even interest, inevitably produced growing opposition to and ultimate rejection of both experiments, discredited without having any real chance of success. The morale of the staff — already low — had taken another severe and needless buffeting and mutual recriminations were abundant when the experiments were abandoned after some ten weeks.

The adoption of mixed ability grouping as the basis of a school's organisational pattern is not simply a physical change, a mere reorganisation of the intake of a school into units which have a different intellectual make-up from their predecessors. The mechanical change is the most easy to accomplish. It is the necessary accompanying adaptation of attitude and re-appraisal of often long practised teaching methods that are far more difficult. These factors, allied to the relative autonomy of teachers within the classroom, demand that any attempt to introduce mixed ability groups which is to have a chance of success must be done with the support of those involved, rather than in their teeth. It is not sufficient to timetable a teacher with unstreamed groups if he or she is then going to teach to the average and in so doing frustrate the majority.

Where does a school start to implement plans for embracing mixed ability grouping which do not command wide support amongst staff? I accept that in terms of the broader implications of mixed ability work — any limited experiments are going to achieve little. Nevertheless many teachers do need reassurance that such groups are not going to lead to classroom riot and immediately declining standards. To have no streaming in some subject areas and streaming (even if it is euphemistically called setting) in others may certainly be counter-productive. Teachers Peter and Paul could well offset each other, the one seeking to raise the self concepts and aspirations of all, the other raising the ambitions of some pupils, and consequently depressing those of others. But if all take a step in the dark and many are not even convinced that they are heading in the right direction, the result can be hysteria. Let a few shine a torch and the remainder may be reassured.

There is no bar to allowing some subjects to experiment in limited fields. In this way, those who have accepted the inherent dangers of streaming and who feel that they can successfully attain their own Departmental objectives when their pupils are not in streamed situations will be given an opportunity to prove their point and become aware of all the problems posed. Of course, optimally, one would hope that in a staff participatory school preliminary discussions would have brought sufficient agreement to enable the undertaking of an experiment across a year group or in an integrated programme in a restricted field such as the Humanities. But the pathways to educational change are rarely so clear of obstacles. Furthermore, whatever the degree of prior preparation, discussion and forethought undertaken by teachers, the real situation always throws up the unexpected — sometimes of a minor nature, but sometimes demanding a total rethinking of method. So, if possible, staff should not be placed in the situation of having to grapple with too many problems at once. At Radyr, for example, newly appointed teachers in 1972-3 had to face the difficulties posed by settling children, aged eleven to fourteen, from seventeen different schools, into a new community which had no procedural patterns established, as well as introducing mixed ability work in all three year groups. It was a tribute to their courage and industry that the only casualty in the initial year was a member of staff who gave in her resignation as her husband's occupation took him from the area! To compile work sheets, for example, for three years in one subject department for a Head of Department who had no colleague in the first session was a phenomenal task — particularly in the first involvement with such an organisation. Mistakes were made of course, and corrected, but the physical pressure understandably affected mental energy and initiative.

Two ways of helping teachers are worthy of mention here. At Radyr the timetable initially provided an escape hatch for staff who found that they were unable to cope with the demands of a radically different teaching situation. The six form intake was divided into six pastoral units, each of which represented a total cross-section of the year group, named, unimaginatively perhaps, after compass points to which no hierarchical order could be ascribed. Then, for each lesson Form groups were timetabled in pairs or threes. Thus, for French 1 North and 1 South worked with their two teachers at the same time. Where there was only one subject teacher in a department, those subject lessons were paired with a similar subject discipline. For example, 1 East had Geography whilst 1 West had History, and vice versa. This at least gave teachers the opportunity to set across a pair of forms if they so desired. Staff were urged to give the new situation a fair chance to establish itself and ultimately only French and Welsh in the latter part of the session with Second Year classes, and Mathematics and Science in the Third Forms took advantage of the possibilities. Setting in our case perhaps only marginally reduced the spread of abilities when putting together two form groups; if whole or half-year groups were blocked together, then more homogeneous units might result − perhaps!

Building such escape routes into a timetable might well be attacked on the grounds that they will be only too easily used. Of course this is a danger, yet it is a risk which must be run. The crucial factor is to convince teachers first and then to bolster confidence by allowing for the possibility of retreat in case of emergency. Teachers must be involved in the decisions which are paramount in importance in their teaching situation − ultimately, anyway, they will take the real decisions within whatever framework is set up − the decisions that are evident at classroom level.

Another essential element in ensuring that teachers are given every chance of success in a different teaching environment is to devote much attention to the composition of mixed ability form units. The term 'mixed ability' should not mean mere random scattering of children amongst classes, using alphabetical order or any similar inconsequential guide line which can have the fortuitous consequence of achieving behavioural, social or academic imbalance in classes. The frightening vision of half a class of non-readers or of troublemakers must be removed. How? Clearly here we are dependent on the information provided by our feeder Primary Schools. Our first meeting with headteachers and assistants was clearly exploratory: we wanted to make ourselves, our school, our objectives known to colleagues whose efforts with our annual addition of two hundred children were to exert much control over our first work with them. We wanted to establish avenues for two-way communication, for our academic and pastoral staff to visit contributory schools and for their teachers to visit us, for Primary School children to come to us and use our facilities, get to know the school and see it at work before they crossed

the Primary-Secondary School divide. We also wanted information and jointly devised a means of briefly recording
the elements we needed to guide us in the composition of
Form tutor groups. So, in May, prior to their entering
Secondary School, top class Juniors receive a visit from their
new year Tutor or Head of School and provide him with
written lists of children with whom they would like to be
associated in their new school. The questionnaire takes the
form: 'If you were given the choice of which boys or girls
you would like to join in your new Form at Radyr name the
three children you would most like to be with.' The pupils'
choice is then linked with information from the Primary
School 'top class teacher'. It tells us very crudely the overall
capabilities of the children on a three point scale (markedly
above average, average, well below average) and whether any
of the youngsters ought to have some form of remedial
treatment in either Mathematics or English.

Despite our joint discussions, the yardsticks will, of course,
vary but this matters little. The capability measure may be
rough but minor discrepancies do not gum up the works.
Their aim is to produce groups with no preponderance or
absence of high fliers or low achievers. Recommendations for
remedial treatment are usually the consequence of a Primary
School's own cut-off line; this is subjectively decided (often
on the basis of staffing facilities or lack of them) by the
individual school. The recommendations are not accepted
without our own additional screening. But, most often, our
tests underline the need for extra help and we are able to get
to grips with the problems of these pupils early, without their
suffering for a period in all mainstream lessons and striving to
readjust many times a day to all the new adults they meet.
Armed then with pupils' friendship choices, guidance about
their achievement levels from teachers who know them
closely, forewarned verbally during our visits about children
who are likely to give most cause for concern behaviourally,
we feel able to produce groups in which children know and
like some of their peers from the first and in which teachers
are not — by mere coincidence — faced by an inordinate
number of behavioural and academic problems at a time
when children are also grappling with the difficulties involved

in adjusting to a new teaching situation.

Just as it is essential that we should be honest with staff and with those who are responsible for the Primary School years of our children, so too must we be honest with parents. By honesty I mean not simply probity but the laying of all cards on the table with regard to organisation and the intentions which underlie it. Education is, of course, a process that is not only the responsibility of the school: pupils' approach to the school and its offerings is largely consequent upon parental attitudes. If teachers are worried about handling unstreamed groups is it not even more certain that parents who have gone through the system will be even more concerned — especially as those who are the most articulate could well feel that they have succeeded *because* of this system? Public relations are important here, and parents respect honesty. Parents — through their Parents', or Parent-Teacher, Association, newsletters, open meetings, specimen teaching lessons, talks by Heads of Department — must be told why such changes are introduced. Many, perhaps, will not be convinced. A friend of mine, whose daughter attended a school at which I taught, accepted the argument for de-streaming but was sure that practical problems would be insuperable and refused to be converted — until his daughter gained six distinctions in her nine Ordinary Level Pass Certificate! Nevertheless, a school is more likely to gain support by airing the subject, explaining principles and avoiding misconceptions and misunderstandings, discussing problems and facing up to arguments than by rejecting parental efforts to gain reassurance that their children's talents are to be fostered and nurtured.

Open discussion with parents is also imperative if they are to be taken into real partnership with the school in the work it is attempting to undertake. It has been suggested earlier that one consequence of the introduction of mixed ability work is the need to re-appraise traditional methods of assessment, evaluation and reporting. If these means of involving parents in pupil progress are to have any impact or significance, adults outside the school must clearly understand the language in which they are couched. Now that the school's valuation of their children is not to be self-evident —

by the stream in which they are placed, by the marks they get, by the positions in class to which they are allotted — parents must be able to understand the criteria of progress that are being used. The school can make such preparations at the macro level. But in order for all pupils, parents and staff to be involved in the change in a real, contributory sense and for problems to be reduced, there is much to be done, too, at the Faculty or Departmental level. My experience — and that of many of my colleagues — was that the first need was to review the teaching objectives. Many times I have been asked whether it was necessary to change what I tried to achieve with children. The question was often put more basically, as an enquiry whether the content of courses became diluted. More basically still, it was asserted that it was fine to teach Social History in this way but the questioner would wager that I had given up Political History! I could heartily refute both suggestions, but the denial is both superficial and irrelevant. As teachers our thoughts are often so dominated by the content of our work that we forget the skill elements which should surely be its core. Is it mischievous to suggest that a vast proportion of subject content is anyway forgotten by children within a short time of learning it or, at least, within a short time after an examination. Discuss with any Sixth Formers their memories of Ordinary Level work in any of the disciplines they have not kept up for Advanced Level for a denunciation of our fact-seeking, regurgitation-demanding public examinations. Before reviewing course content, teaching methods or modes of assessment in our Departments, we must carefully analyse what we are trying to do and consider our priorities.

This would appear to make an arrogant assumption — that those who teach streamed classes have not thought out what they are doing whilst those who have accepted the need for heterogeneous groupings have seen a great light! This seeming slight on many able and honest teachers is not intended, but such a searching appraisal of aims certainly made a significant difference in my own case, and in that of many of my former and present colleagues. For me this crucial analysis of my work came much later than it should have done, and for some time I was blinded by my fear that I was merely making a rationalisation about the practice I had developed. This was probably partly true but, nevertheless it did result in my overt acceptance of several key objectives which I had either formerly only accepted unconsciously or which just hadn't dawned on me. Objectives will not be attained by accident; failure to use them as one's springboard in any curriculum, in any attempt to devise a syllabus, or learning experiences, teaching methods or assessment techniques will be counter-productive.

To illustrate this at Departmental level: the Historian must ask what is the relative importance of teaching the facts about the events that happened in the Battle of Marston Moor in 1644 and of teaching ways of finding out about these facts and reporting them. Again, which to *him* (and this is important, for all teaching is idiosyncratic) and his Departmental colleagues is more important — to stimulate pupils' interest in History or to increase their knowledge of History? These and a host of similar questions about where we are going must be answered before we decide which road we are going to take in terms of content or approach. It was in this way that a working party recently established at Radyr to examine the possibility of developing an integrated course in the Humanities found that the overlap of intention held by specialists in English, Geography and History in the first year of Secondary School courses was so great that it would be folly to ask eleven year olds to readjust to several personalities and learning environments in a week when each of these teachers was concerned with promoting the same skills.

Once objectives have been recognised and declared, content areas and resource availability can be reviewed. But let us beware of moving on to this stage without really delving into the vital discussion of objectives. We must think in operational terms — what do we really want pupils to be able to do, not only ultimately but at various stages in their school careers? If we want them to be interested in our subject, we must devise learning experiences likely to contribute towards this. If we wish our children to write or think quickly (as many of our external examinations seem to wish), we must structure courses which help them develop these skills.

When objectives — and even their hierarchical ordering — are decided, then content areas and approaches to teaching can be decided with greater validity. The probability is that most of what has formerly been taught will continue to be offered to pupils. Clearly, however, with the much changed composition of teaching groups, methods must be adapted and this can affect or be affected by a whole host of things: timetabling, resources and teacher skills, for example. Any decision to undertake team teaching or integration of subject disciplines hitherto working in isolation must obviously mean the blocking of certain teachers and classes together in the timetable. Less obvious, perhaps, is the need to study the time units normally available for lessons in a given school.

Whilst a traditional didactic approach of chalk and talk tends to result in teacher (and pupil) preference for short periods of time, in many subjects the accepted pattern of five minutes' revision, ten minutes' exposition, twenty minutes' consolidation could well become inappropriate. Where these teaching techniques are going to be abandoned, the single lesson unit ought to be closely examined. If children are not to be programmed to do the same things at the same time, classroom organisation is more problematic. If a variety of approaches to work is going to be encouraged or even built into programmes, the single short lesson of thirty to forty minutes can become an unwelcome constraint. Movement to a specialist room at the end of a single lesson, the collection by children then of the numerous learning aids and materials they may individually be using, the distribution of marked folders or exercise books, and the return later of all these can literally take up to one third of a lesson. Many teachers will therefore think in terms of double lessons — thus halving the problem of pupil movement and of distribution and collection of materials whilst enabling the use of film or locality-based work without regular disturbance of the lessons of others who teach the class for other single periods before or after their lesson.

Whilst the double lesson unit has these undoubted attractions, other problems result from its introduction. Modern Language specialists will understandably seek to continue to

administer their 'daily dose' in short sharp bursts, though
some research is beginning to challenge the assumption that
this is necessarily the most efficient way of attaining
proficiency in a language. In some schools, where there is
little or no extraction of children needing remedial attention,
it might be felt that for these children concentration in one
subject area for two lessons might be creating, rather than
solving, problems. Where these problems are felt widely in a
given school, a solution may be found in the adoption of
one-hour units in the day. In others, problems can be solved
in more individual ways. For example, whilst most lessons are
taught in double period units, it is still possible to have single
lessons for languages where two are taught. French and Welsh
or German classes can be paired and taught in the same
physical area of the school. At the end of a single period it is
then a relatively easy matter either for teachers to move a
short distance from one class to another or for classes to
move across from one specialist room to another. Another
possibility is the suggestion made earlier that Subject
Departments wishing for double lessons in a basically single
lesson pattern of timetable may have pairs of forms (or their
multiples) taught at the same time and then agree mutually
to teach half of the grouping exclusively for one subject in
half-term (or more or less) cycles. Thus, a combination of
Religious Education and Geography for this purpose may
result in Form 2Y being taught two double periods of R.E.
per week for eight weeks instead of their usual two single
periods, whilst 2X have the same allotment of Geography.
The following eight weeks of term will then see 2Y studying
Geography and 2X meeting the R.E. specialist for two double
periods every week.

Again, for the minority time subjects in the Lower School
(that is, those lessons like Geography, History, Religious
Education and Music, whose teachers might only be allocated
two lessons per week with each Form) the adoption of the
double lesson unit can also create a problem in that they will
only see pupils once a week. Yet this argument seems to be
one in which losses on the roundabout are offset by gains on
the swings. Some have accepted the virtues of the lengthier
lesson unit on the grounds already indicated, but they have

also suggested that it is difficult to develop a meaningful relationship with children in one session a week, that children find it hard to pick up the strands of what they are doing after a lapse of seven days (and one day's absence can cause this lapse of time to be a fortnight). Both points are contestable. Are relationships developed by the frequency of meetings between teacher and learner or by the quality of those meetings? Single lessons will either lead to a hurried whistle-stop tour of all children or, more desirably surely, a development of a work situation wherein children work more infrequently with a teacher as an individual — the work being structured for individual progress — but for lengthier periods at a time, enabling a better qualitative interaction between the two. Is the lapse of time so important when the individual child is involved personally and in a real way in the structuring and development of his own work? This factor, linked with the homework session which, when a single week's lesson is in operation, may well be spread over two or three evenings, might well overcome the problem.

Whatever decision is taken by the Department, however, it is clearly one which warrants thought — and early — for so many others must be consulted, including whoever is responsible for timetabling and other Departments which could be affected by any proposed change. At the same time, other resources must be considered. As methods of teaching are discussed it is essential to avoid constraints which may be placed on teachers not only by the time factor but also by the space element. The school in which I now teach includes an area designed for use by the First Forms in full recognition of the fact that the youngsters who would use these rooms would be faced by what could be severe problems for many as they tried to adjust from a school situation where they remained in one room with one teacher for the greater part of their time to the exact antithesis of this. To minimise this problem the suite of rooms was built in three pairs, each equipped with work-tops, movable tables, water, gas taps and folding partitions between them to admit of large group work and team teaching organisation as desired. Yet the admirable vision which saw First Year children remaining in their room bases for a large part of their timetable proved to be impossible to translate into practical terms when teaching mixed ability groups. Subject room bases proved to be essential, given the host of materials that could be used in any one lesson. In very few subjects do children now carry one textbook each for the whole of the year (even if we could afford that). Each pupil could use several books even in one lesson, let alone on one topic. Each class will need a great assortment of other items — scissors, glue, card, paper, paint, brushes, stapler, slide viewer, polyfilla, plasticine, wood — and these cannot easily be carted all over the school. The provision of wheeled trolleys may help the situation, but only a limited selection can be moved in this way; the subject room, or rooms, are a prerequisite of effective teaching, whether in a streamed or mixed ability situation.

Clearly, too, teaching methods to be embraced by a Department must be discussed at length. Herein lies the problem of marrying together the need to deal with each individual in a group of varying abilities with making the maximum use of various types of expertise of staff available. There is always a danger that in over-structuring in order to deal with the first, the method will stifle the initiative and spark of the individual teacher. Whilst it is paramount to undertake careful preparation, beware of over rigidity: it might not be responsive to pupil interests or changed teacher attitudes which become apparent as a course progresses. Nevertheless, it is necessary to agree broad general principles of approach. Even if members of a given Department agree to differ they must talk through their individual methods of trying to achieve their corporate goals — if only to ensure that their ideas are subjected to analysis and criticism by colleagues who might reveal inherent dangers hitherto unrealised.

Most methods encountered in dealing with mixed ability groups tend to be heuristic rather than didactic: pupils are stimulated to find their own way along a path where the teacher has placed signposts and on stretches of which he will act as guide. Here, again, several questions must be raised before entering into work with unstreamed classes. What is the teacher's rôle in this situation? To what degree is work to be individualised? Is classwork, in the sense of the whole group working together at the same thing with the teacher as the focal point, to be totally abandoned? If not, for what purposes and at what stages can this method be used? Is the grouping of children within the classroom as mini-teaching or learning units to be encouraged? If so, on what criteria? If work is to be individualised, how are assignment sheets or work paths to be devised? Will they be composed by individuals or by groups of teachers? On what principles should they be developed? The list of questions demanding preliminary discussion is a lengthy one.

The reaction of a student on teaching practice to his first encounter with a mixed ability class was quite natural. His own experiences of education had been in a traditional, highly selective, single-sex Grammar School and at University. He had been talked *at* throughout his career and though he had discussed the problems of individualising work with several competent teachers, though he liked and carefully worked at a work sheet approach, the implications of such a teaching method had not really reached him till he entered into the work situation. With a somewhat stunned expression he announced that he felt that as a teacher he was redundant! His stimulus session over, his work sheet explained, he then felt that, apart from answering the odd question or two, he had nothing to do.

It is easy to laugh off such a reaction, easy to attribute it to the fact that this student had been remote from little children for a long time and that it would take time to cross the age barrier and relate again to youngsters as individuals. Such a response would, however, be misguided, for, to a lesser extent perhaps, it is a problem that faces all teachers. To change one's role from a relatively remote lecturer, in front of the class, opening to them gateways to learning via an experience they all undergo, to that of a partner in learning, of an adviser, a critic at an individual level is not easy. The contrast is exaggerated here, perhaps, but the challenge to the security of teachers is nevertheless a real one. In practical terms what do we do in a classroom? Answers will, of course, be idiosyncratic, depending on objectives. But we must agree on what we will seek to do in this situation:

ensure that our pupils are not merely copying or regurgitating lengthy gobbets from source materials (an inherent criticism of the work situation we have created), question and probe about what the children write (suggestions are better given in face to face situations than via comments at the foot of marked work, necessary complements to discussion though these may be), stimulate pupils to ask supplementary questions themselves or to consult sources not hitherto suggested, act as consultant about media to be used in dealing with problems, discuss misconceptions or inadequacies noted when marking. Whichever our priorities may be, teachers — particularly inexperienced teachers — must discuss their approaches beforehand. In this way traumatic experiences may be avoided!

Clearly, many groups of teachers will decide to use assignment or work sheets in order to provide work at manifold levels to meet the challenge of classes whose members vary in intelligence and attainment levels, degrees of motivation and interest. Once this decision is taken, two possible approaches commend themselves. Work for the first term might then be split amongst the members of a Department according to their interests. Each might thus undertake to plan the stimulus lesson and subsequent assignments for one topic. This certainly minimises the work load for members of staff and enables each to indulge his own interest, in his own way. A weakness here appears to lie in the inefficiency of the method in that although it does capitalise on the opportunity to make reality of principles of work-sharing it concurrently only allows the team to benefit from the skills of all the team over a lengthy period of time as completed work packs are presented for discussion. Simultaneous preparation of packs by several teachers tends to result in work in isolation, liaison and feed-back from colleagues only coming when the work is complete (maybe at draft stage, maybe even at publication stage) and when alterations are not readily or easily made. Ideas are communicated more slowly in this way — often only as a consequence of working through sheets with classes — and teachers often find it difficult to use someone else's packs without going through all the thinking and planning stages.

It is preferable, therefore, for all to be involved in the early stages if possible, whilst still seeking not to impose too heavy a burden on anyone. Clearly the statement of objectives and agreement about the learning experiences most likely to achieve these goals must be the result of a consensus; the teacher's autonomy can otherwise doom so many intentions from the start. Thereafter units of work may be devised for individuals or pairs to work on, but, at each stage, the opinions of other members of the team should be formally sought (it's too easy to overlook individuals otherwise). Thus a pair may offer for discussion its sub-unit titles, its stimulus lessons for each sub-unit, its work sheets or modes of evaluation, to ascertain whether the goals have been achieved. It is only through discussion that the thinking behind each section can be revealed, deficiencies found, remedies suggested, ideas passed on. This seems in most ways to provide the basic elements of team teaching in a more real sense than the final alternative which may commend itself to teachers. Here, teachers may in turn teach stimulus lessons via lecture, film, chalk and talk, display, tape-assisted talk or the twin focus teaching medium, using two teachers in a discussion situation — a salutary experience for team members as well as pupils. From this springboard, friendship groups, pastoral groups or interest groups may then go to different members of the teaching team, according to the follow-up topic they are offering, or always to the same teacher who will devise his follow-up to the initial offering as he wishes. Alternatively, children may rotate round teacher groups. Several permutations are possible, according to whatever objectives have been set. In a Modern Language the initial audio-visual lesson might be delivered by one of the team, and subsequent lessons in the unit might then vary in the classrooms of each other member of the teaching team. In a Social Studies unit an opening lesson, discussing the theme of Towns, might be followed-up along a host of different paths, historically, geographically or locally based. This method preserves the individuality of the teachers' approach towards the attaining of agreed ends but, at the same time, it appears to lose so many of the possible advantages offered by working in a teaching team.

Whichever method is adopted, the ubiquitous work sheet is likely to make its appearance. What principles should be considered in its writing? Again one must return to basic tenets. What are we trying to achieve in our teaching? Whether it is the gleaning of information, the independent gathering of such material, the understanding of such material, the application of principles discovered to new situations or the stimulation of the imagination through the use of facts provided or found, these aims must be enshrined in the work set. Such a statement seems somewhat trite and obvious but it is so easy to become bogged down in one element of one's work, such as the accumulation of fact in any historical study.

Whatever one's goals, however, the work sheet must be designed to allow all pupils to be fully taxed. This demands an attempt to introduce tasks which, through the sheet, progress from the simple to the complex, from the closed to the open. Throughout, the sheet must be couched in simple, direct language – this does not mean that all tasks set are simple, of course, but it does ensure that all can at least understand what is expected from them. If, for example, in a language work is being done on the future tense might not assignments progress from simple replication exercises from a model given (that is using the same endings with different verbs) to the completion of sentences wherein the infinitive of the verb is given for amendment to the writing of sentences or a paragraph of a child's own devising? At each stage additional information might be provided as more complex tasks are demanded – this will perhaps be particularly true in Mathematics. Similarly, in History, Geography or Religious Education sheets can advance through progressively more difficult tasks. Initially, children might be asked to establish certain basic facts: Who led the Armada? With what objective? Where was it to link with additional military support? . . . Then pupils might be asked to use the information built up in a novel context – a radio interview, a wall newspaper, a series of maps or illustrations, a log book – to show that they have understood the researched information. Basic material will be available in the relatively simple texts or source material, more detail will be located in more sophisticated, available resources. Thus, each child has a challenge to answer by the open nature of the later tasks.

At different stages — according to the maturity of the pupils or their previous experience — references may be more or less specific, giving page of chapter references or not, giving book titles and authors or not. Indeed, I have even experimented with asking children to write their own sheet assignments after giving mere references to topics such as the Fire of London.

A few words of warning ought perhaps to be spoken here. Work sheets, with pupils soon at various stages in them, can pose problems of resources, of how to apply a final cut off time and even of tedium. The first is of course partly the perennial problem of finance, of having sufficient resources to cope with all the many added demands on the Departmental exchequer as a consequence of the introduction of mixed ability work. Shelves of individual readers cannot be built up overnight, nor slideviewers and the large amounts of soft ware each Department needs be collected through a couple of years' requisitions. Parents' Associations, sponsoring this or that enterprise, can help ease the shortage situation. So too can requests not to block too many classes in a given year group together or to timetable the study of topics to try to ensure that too many classes are not concentrating on one at the same time. Is there any reason why 1Z should not be studying coordinates in Mathematics whilst 1M is working at symmetry or why the one should not be working in the field of local Geology whilst the other is looking at map-reading in Geography? Again, it is prior planning that is called for.

Clearly, when children are all working at the same work sheet, some are likely to make more rapid progress than others. What happens when some finish whilst some are still in mid sheet? Does this matter? Is it right to cut the latter off, their work incomplete? Again, the answer lies in the construction of the work sheet, with any subject matter which it is crucial that all should deal with being introduced in the early assignments. Just as these move from simple to complex and from closed to open, so they should develop from the crucial to the peripheral, from the mastery of basic material to studies in depth. This can be done within one sheet or with basic and follow-up sheets and so closure can be applied with adequate warning when all have grappled with the preliminary essentials.

It is all too easy to become overcome by teaching methods or by pegs to teaching about the value of which one is convinced. I once heard a boy of low ability threaten never again to ride in a car! This was the consequence of the generous gift of two old cars to the school. Thus, those who would today be called Newsom children used the cars as the base for their Mathematics, studying running costs, depreciation and so forth. In Social Studies the history of the car and the nature of the motor car industry were followed-up. Science lessons were for a time devoted to the functioning of our vehicles and Craft lessons were spent in putting them in running order. Soon the lesson stimulus became such a bore that the boys looked forward to lessons in which it was very difficult to study automobiles in any shape or form! In like manner changes in teachers' approaches to lessons are welcome to pupils who enjoy working independently or with their neighbours for a large part of the time. The discussion of topics, the study of work done, a class lesson to pull together various strands of a work sheet, reporting back by different study groups, all are welcome breaks in routine which children relish the more because they are different. Indeed I never really worked out whether one of my pupils was being flattering or accusatory when she said, 'I love working at sheets, sir, but it's nice to hear you teach for a change'!

8 'What about the Remedials?'

'How can I use work sheets when half of my class can't read?' 'Surely the least able children must hold back those who are bright?' These questions — or some variant of them — must be the ones most frequently met in discussing mixed ability grouping with teachers. Both are very proper questions, both rooted in pictures of ill-motivated bottom streamers, with the constant problems of disruption they have posed, being placed in the same classroom as able youngsters who have accepted the school's goals and are working earnestly towards them.

Two answers that could be suggested are valid but unsatisfactory. Even allowing for the exaggeration which is usual when defining a problem, it must be said that a class with a high number of non-readers is hardly a class of mixed ability in its proper sense. Whilst the classroom situation rarely provides a mirror image of the theorists' conception of it nevertheless one would anticipate a spread of ability loosely following a normal distribution curve of intelligence, with the bulk of children excluded from the two extremes. If a large number of pupils in one class are non-readers then it is not the problem of mixed ability work that faces the teacher, rather is it one of devising a programme or pattern of organisation which sets out to inculcate basic literacy skills. It must be stressed that to derive maximum benefit from a mixed ability situation classes must contain a fair share of able children from an all-ability intake. Criticisms based on experience in a Secondary Modern School, for example, where — by definition — all children have been crudely labelled as failures, are hardly tenable. Similarly, Grammar School experiences can be misleading guides. I developed an inferiority complex within a quarter of an hour of listening to a course colleague describing some of the universal

achievements of his First Form mixed ability class whom he
still taught basically by chalk and talk. It was only when he
revealed that he taught in a highly selective Grammar School
that my self-respect was restored! Too often suspicions and
fears have arisen from lack of knowledge about the normative
system; it is understandable that teachers taking a step into
the unknown – for example, from Grammar to Comprehensive School – might exaggerate the problems they expect
to await them, but the grounds and validity of the criticism
or fear must always be examined.

In the same way it is not easy to convince a teacher who
has spent all his career in a streamed situation that nature can
be defied and that the leopard can change his spots. Knowing
grins often meet the assertion that the bottom streamer as we
have long known him is comparatively rarely in evidence in
an established mixed ability situation. Research work quoted
to back up personal experience is often countered by the
example of a pupil, frequently from a broken home,
generally below average in intelligence, invariably from a
non-supportive working-class background, often physically
over developed, who has been a pain-in-the-neck for teachers
and the idol of his mates since he left the Primary School.
Will mixed ability grouping suddenly make him amenable?
Stranger things have happened! Of course, one cannot
counter arguments based on specific cases from a highly
idiosyncratic situation, but it can nevertheless be suggested
that – despite factors that are extraneous to the educational
system – such children often develop their behaviour pattern
as the consequence of the experiences, based on rejection, to
which we subject them in our schools. Problems and problem
children do continue to exist in an unstreamed situation, but
it is my contention that they are very definitely minimised
and not restricted largely to one ability band (a fact which
was hitherto all too damaging of a system which was based
on the early rejection of some of our children).

Indeed, I sometimes wonder if non-streaming highlights
problems that previously we didn't even realise existed, such
as the under-taxing and under-performing of many of our
youngsters. Due to our assumptions about the homogeneity
of our streamed groups, we taught our classes, naturally, at

one level (though we never put this into words): probably to the average child of the class. As a consequence, how many of our most able were under-stretched as they quietly and diligently went through the basic tasks we set in common for all? Perhaps I exaggerate — certainly some teachers were alive to this and structured their work accordingly, but how many? If work is individualised — in whatever way — it presupposes that children have different potentialities in every topic, let alone in every subject. Artificial ceilings of achievement must not be imposed on any child; each must be allowed — indeed pressed — to reach his or her own limits of achievement. The careful structuring of assignments — by their open-endedness, their progression from basic to depth studies, from easy to difficult and their allowance for branching programmes of follow-up studies to linear bases — should thus allow for the extending of all pupils, regardless of the spread of ability in a class.

Yet, in some ways, these answers are not acceptable, based as they are on the ideal situation in the first instance and on subjective experience in the second. Though the problem of Secondary pupils needing remedial attention can be all too easily overstated, it does exist. For a host of reasons, any truly comprehensive intake to a Secondary School will contain amongst its numbers some children whose performance of the basic elements of literacy and numeracy is inadequate. Should these be winkled out from the first, placed in a separate group with specialist remedial staff and allowed to follow a course devised especially for them? Should this be a temporary measure with the objective of returning pupils to a full main stream lesson situation as soon as it is thought that they can cope with this? Can their needs be fully met within the mixed ability context?

What are our aims when working with these children? Clearly all would point out that our first duty is to help the least able of our pupils to master the basic skills of reading, writing, speaking and counting. In the crudest of senses they must be mastered if these youngsters are to be able to cope with so many of life's problems. If they are to meet the demands of society they must be able to fill in forms, check their wages and bills, read letters they receive, ask for guidance or direction. But is this all? They will live in a mixed ability society; should not schools prepare them for that society? One of the arguments advanced for the introduction of comprehensivisation was that such schools would provide microscosms of society at large. It was felt that to stratify secondary education within the tripartite divisions of Secondary Modern, Technical and Grammar Schools was to create the bases of a similarly stratified society, with little contact between or understanding of one element by another. Yet to organise a Comprehensive School in which the opportunities for establishing this contact and understanding are minimised or reduced to the accidental is surely wasteful? The presence of children of varying intelligence, background and interest on the same school campus will not ensure their intermingling in any meaningful way unless our organisation is geared to bring this about. If our aim is to prepare children to participate in society in the fullest sense we must give them the opportunity to meet and to understand the behaviour patterns, standards, interests and ambitions of others who form part of that same society. This is surely important for all children, regardless of intelligence or background?

Believing that schools must be agents of socialisation as well as being responsible for the development of the skills of literacy and numeracy, I feel unhappy about the total extraction of pupils for remedial treatment. The motives underlying the creation of remedial departments with their own permanent staff and clientèle are of course unexceptionable. It is maintained that the least able of our children need much time with one person to build up a worthwhile working relationship which will enable them to benefit from the expertise of skilled, specially trained, sympathetic teachers. Subject teachers in a demanding large-class situation will be unable to give these children the help they need because of time pressures and because, by the nature of their teaching programme, they will rarely come into contact with these youngsters and hardly be able to build up a meaningful interaction in the few periods per week allocated to that subject. Yet does the system of total extraction only meet one of the suggested objectives — the inculcation of basic

skills? Is it right to cocoon children in their own little world,
then, at the age of sixteen, to throw them into a society so
many parts of which they have not yet experienced? Is this
not to create societal and school problems? However well-
intentioned are the plans to adopt a policy of positive
discrimination to help the less able — whether we call them
remedial children, Newsom group or R O S L A forms — they
are still likely to face problems if they isolate a group, as
rejects. Surely the greater the degree of separation — by
composition of the group, staffing, physical provision (suite
of rooms or whatever) or curriculum — the greater the degree
of isolation, sense of identity and introspection, and creation
of group norms which are alien to those of others (to the
G C E band or to the C S E band perhaps)? This is counter-
productive in the educational terms suggested above and
often in behavioural terms, as so often demonstrated in
traditional bottom streams.

For many years some schools have sought to meet such
problems by part time extraction of the whole group of
pupils needing remedial attention. Thus, they will be scattered across the whole year group when placed initially in
forms under the care of a form tutor. This group will be a
permanent unit which for three, four or five years will be
registered together, have joint responsibilities such as acting
as service form to the school in a given week or taking
assembly, act together in social competition — inter-form
quizzes, displays, games leagues — and whose needs will be
the concern of the form tutor having responsibility for
helping with their problems and keeping their records. These
mixed ability units are retained for certain lessons — in my
experience, Art, Handicraft, Housecraft, Music, Physical
Education and, curiously, Religious Education (perhaps areas
where work has long since been individualised or cooperative
work is essential?). For all other lessons the year group will
then be setted into more homogeneous groups. In this way,
children of all abilities might work together for perhaps a
quarter of their time at school.

Several benefits may accrue from the adoption of such a
pattern of organisation. As it is usual for the same teacher or
perhaps pair of teachers to take the bottom set across all the

academic areas deemed suitable for the least able children, these youngsters will not come into contact with so many teachers or have to readjust to different patterns of teaching so often. Specially trained teachers will help them concentrate on putting basic weaknesses right whilst, at the same time, they will have the opportunities to meet and work with their more able peers and to benefit from this interaction situation.

Very clearly this pattern of organisation has much to commend it, contributing greatly towards the achievement of both academic and social objectives. Yet it may be argued that it minimises rather than removes problems, fails to capitalise totally on the opportunities presented by a mixed ability situation and creates some problems too. In accepting this approach all too often we accept the pessimistic view that once a child is designated to be in need of remedial attention so he will always remain. Thus, for example, during the 'setted' sessions the lowest ability band might not be allowed to study French or Welsh on the grounds that their needs are more basic. Again, the content of their courses in the setted subjects may be so watered down as to admit of no future return to main stream lessons. This seems to preach a doctrine of despair, to fatalistically accept that the child's fate is already sealed, a view which is hardly likely to provide children with an incentive to succeed in their present situation.

Furthermore, the halfway house nature of this system can be counter-productive to our aim of socialisation. Personal observation would support researched findings that children at the extremes of the intelligence and attainment spectra rarely befriend each other, but, even so, friendship patterns are unpredictable and by no means regularly limited to one level of intelligence. To place children in a mixed ability unit for only twenty-five per cent of their time and with a segregated group for the remaining sessions is almost to guarantee the forming of sub-cultures based on the common group timetable. That is, 'remedial children' — together for most of their school time — will only befriend each other and find it difficult to break into the established friendship patterns of their more able peers in the relatively short time

they spend together. When Ellen, Mary and Jean go to all
their school lessons together, is it not probable that they will
also spend much of their free time together and reject the
efforts of Dawn, whom they see for only a few lessons, to
break into their circle?

If, then, the full-time and part-time group extraction
systems present problems, although to a markedly greater or
lesser extent, can one envisage a situation in which there is no
extraction of groups for remedial work except on an ad hoc
basis? I have seen this work successfully, but it is questionable to advance this system as universally workable. At
Settle, at one stage, itinerant remedial help was brought into
the mainstream classroom, with a pair of teachers operating
in harness, using carefully devised assignments wherein every
pupil was guided to tasks with which he or she could cope
initially via the use of resources suited to his or her
capabilities. This solution is admirable but it is totally
dependent on two factors — a relatively small number
(perhaps two per form) of children needing remedial aid and
the availability of a large amount of remedial staff help.
Though Settle's intake included many children of low
attainment there were comparatively few annually who
arrived at the school barely able to read — a possible result of
the fact that very many attended small Primary Schools with
a good pupil-teacher ratio that contributed to the marked
progress attendant upon much individual attention. Thus,
when there was a declared need for help in several classrooms
at the same time, the problem could often be overcome by
timetabling the remedial teacher for one of the two weekly
History lessons for a given form, for example to set a pupil
on the right path which the subject teacher could reinforce in
short periods, sitting with the child. Some teachers indeed
made use of senior pupil volunteers to help with some of the
tasks like listening to reading or ensuring that work tasks
were understood. Similarly, in inter-disciplinary situations
the addition of an itinerant remedial specialist to a teaching
team, can contribute to the solution of such problems as long
as numbers needing help are not too great.

Few schools, however, can enjoy a situation such as this.
At Radyr the school has accepted both socialising and

academic objectives, though with different emphases at varying stages of the pupils' school careers. Our main goal is to work towards the ultimate placement of all pupils in the main stream situation for all lessons. Thus we try to look at our least able children as individuals and not as a group, and try to programme them accordingly. Here, numbers are larger by the nature of the school — a six-form entry, mixed Comprehensive School on the north west fringes of Cardiff, drawing children from eight Primary Schools in varying environments — farming communities, dormitory suburbs and mining villages. In 1973-4, twenty-four children in the First Forms received some remedial attention, sixteen of these for the maximum amount of time allocated to the Year Group. In the early stages, Years One and Two, the academic aim is stressed, but not at the expense of the total exclusion of pupils receiving remedial treatment from the company of their year group peers. They may be extracted for up to a maximum of about two thirds of the timetable, joining their mixed ability form tutor group for twelve periods of Art, Craft, Drama, Music, P.E. and Games. In their third year — where two Option Groups allow some children to drop one or two languages, others to begin a new language or Rural Science, others to take extra Craft courses — these pupils are integrated to a much greater extent in the predominant timetabling arrangements, being extracted at most for four English and six Mathematics periods. For their last two years of compulsory schooling all children follow courses in English, Physical Education and Personal Relationships (all in mixed ability groups) as in Mathematics (where a half-year group of three forms are setted into four groups). In addition to this common core, each child — together with parents and staff — chooses one subject from each of six multiple choice Option Groups, each containing G C E, C S E and Internal Certificate Choices. Erstwhile Third Form 'remedial children' tend to select Internal Certificate courses in five of the options, but only five (out of sixteen) have this session done so universally. In the last group, in common with seventy-five per cent of their fellows, they make choices from a cycle of half-term Education for Leisure courses.

The essence of the school's philosophy is that children

should increasingly be placed in groups which are not restricted to members of the least able stratum of the school community. At the same time it is felt to be important that they should be able to select their courses rather than that they themselves should be selected out. A minority — some four or five — have found problems in the mixed ability context of the upper school, a couple have faced difficulties which have demanded some flexibility on our part (such as that involved in a change of options), but the majority have derived benefit from working with more able peers and have risen to the challenge and stimulus of working with more teachers than hitherto. In two ways we have attempted to cushion the shock of full transference to the timetable followed by all children in their Fourth Year. In the first place, we have tried to supplement the work of Remedial Department specialists in the Lower School by introducing other teachers to the group for limited periods. Where staff have some slack time (not often!) they have joined Remedial groups to work with individuals — listening to them read, helping them to compensate for absence, administering standardised tests, or merely working in harness with specialists. Religious Education and Physical Education staff have acted in this way as ancillaries in the present session (1973-4), but they could as well have been Mathematicians, Scientists or Craft personnel. Some members of staff are also timetabled for one session weekly with one remedial Year Group or another — The Headmaster and a linguist take French studies, an R.E. specialist introduces her subject, I teach some local Geography and History. In this way we prepare children for meeting with several teachers in the weekly cycle and try to show that they are not regarded as a separate, isolated (rejected) group in the community. It has also been thought advisable to place one Internal Certificate Option in Forms IV and V — Social Studies — in the hands of one of the Remedial Department staff — thus not entirely removing the props that formerly bolstered the efforts of these children and helping to provide an early warning system of any incipient problems which they see looming before them.

Perhaps the most important elements in our approach are

to see each child as an individual, with individual needs, and, however possible, to bolster a morale which is all too sadly very low by the time the age of eleven is reached. Thus, in the same way that individual choice is encouraged at the senior level, so, in junior forms, pupils having remedial attention have almost entirely individual programmes. Some may be extracted from Mathematics only, perhaps just from French, maybe from English, History, Geography and Religious Education, or perhaps from Science and Mathematics. It is the declared intention of the Remedial Department to return their charges to mainstream lessons as soon as it is thought that they will be able to cope without distress. Nothing succeeds like success and, though one or two mistakes have been committed and unhappy pupils sought to return to their original fold, most have flourished as a consequence.

This approach does, of course, create problems, as well as solving them! Crucially, it provides solutions for children; inevitably it leads to problems for staff. In linear subjects, such as Mathematics, there must be some degree of parallelism in the topics pupils have studied (though even here the study of largely self contained topics in the subject makes return of pupils easier than hitherto). Communication between specialist subject staff and the Remedial Department must be close, particularly as to the timing of projected returns. Quite simply — using the Year Tutor (whose role in the school at large is principally to support and coordinate the pastoral work of Form Tutors) as a medium — the Remedial staff complete a form indicating their intention of returning a named child to main stream lessons from a specific date. Subject staff responsible for the group into which the child will return will merely sign the form if this poses no problems or will indicate the need for delay if the intended time of return might make it difficult for the newcomer to be integrated in the group. (In like manner, a Year Tutor — at the instigation of any subject teacher — might seek staff reaction to taking a child from normal lessons to get remedial attention.)

Finally — and, it seems, tritely — headaches are created initially for staff and children when children of limited intelligence have totally individual timetables. There's no one to latch on to, to guide them to one of so many rooms. Is this a chance to play the system, to spend time wandering about from room to room, toilet to toilet? Occasionally we have suspected that. Usually, however, the problem is one of reassuring the worried youngster, who is only too keen to return to lessons with his form mates, one of whom can at the beginning be given the role of guide. Indeed, they sometimes begin to return to lessons they fancy without authority to do so! These are usually only early-session teething problems but they can be an added strain at an already harassing time of year.

How can one evaluate one approach to this problem against another? In all honesty, this can only be done intuitively at this stage. My own feelings, after experience of all the patterns sketched in this chapter, are that early extraction according to individual needs and the increasing integration of students as they progress through the Secondary School achieves objectives I would consider important. The change of emphasis from basic literacy skills to social skills as the child grows older I would defend — if only on pragmatic grounds. If as teachers we have failed to inculcate the former skills in children by the age of fourteen, are we likely to succeed thereafter? As I wrote earlier (p.32), Her Majesty's Inspectors, evaluating a mixed ability experiment at The Woodlands School, Coventry, found hitherto low-stream children 'cooperative and amenable'. My frequent use of 'remedial children' to show visitors round the school in small groups has often been greeted with disbelief by these people when told that their guides were children with severe academic problems in some areas. The children's apparent feeling for their school, together with their frankness and friendliness to these authority figures, regularly gives me added faith in the system we have devised. Children will only learn if they are happy in a given situation; their relative content is encouraging.

9 Marking, Assessing, Reporting

One of my most indelible memories of the Grammar School I attended as a boy is of my desk! It was not its iron framework and heavy, scarred wooden top that endeared it to me but its placement. The six long rows in the classroom each had their significance — four were for boys, two were girls' and we were allotted to them according to performance. The rear right-hand corner seat, like a royal throne, was reserved for the highest male achiever, whilst on this deity's left was the next in line to the succession. The snake of achievement wound its way down the rows; the tail — coiled in that row which sat at the teacher's feet — represented the least active part of that organism and, as if the reptile was a rattlesnake, it had to be watched for nuisancesome activities! And this was the 'A' Form! Yet I didn't object to the system — I revelled in it! Weekly lists, percentages, rank ordering of the class, examinations, hounding the staff for results in the form of a list, adding up marks to get aggregate and average performances and placings, the termly ceremony of moving places — I enjoyed them all. The competitive element stirred me and after all — if the thought really ever did occur to me — this is what education, and indeed life itself, is all about. The school was well thought of, its teachers well qualified and able, it was giving us the best possible start for the competitive outside world.

My friends and I loved it, as I suspect most of us who succeeded in the system did. Of course, the old Grammar Schools had very much to give but for us to leap to their defence on the grounds that they gave us, working-class outsiders from life's main areas of affluence, the chance to rise from our humble beginnings, is dangerous and myopic. Did we succeed due to the system or in spite of it? I stood by the system because it did me well — my desk was in the back row — just! But so were my friends' — there appeared to be a friendship gap after two rows in our class; those beyond the pale were somehow not our sort — yet this was an express stream in a school of successes as adjudged on harsh eleven plus terms. These children were treated — unconsciously I'm sure — as failures and their failure was continually reinforced, even by their desk position. These pupils didn't crowd round displayed mark lists, work out their overall totals, or see it as important if they moved desks: indeed it was rather a nuisance to move one place sideways in the bottom row.

Emotive as such a picture may appear to many readers, does it not, nevertheless, offer to us some warnings about the dangers which can still be inherent in a mixed ability situation? We have sought to avoid selection and rejection, categorisation and stigmatisation, but this is not done merely by removing labels from classes, however far along the way this may help us. When teaching unstreamed groups for the first time marking — in qualitative terms anyway — appeared to be one of the least of problems. I had long believed that children respond to careful, positive marking — a mere tick at the end of three or four pages of thought and effort being both discouraging and depressing, and meriting the decline of standards that will come in its wake. For this reason and to ensure that children's efforts were being maintained in weekly cycles of work, I tried to see everyone's book at seven-day intervals. The mark load was heavy — children working individually in History seem much more prolific in terms of output — to an extent where I confess I wondered whether detailed marking was becoming counter-productive; but, evidently, from early days, a much greater problem existed.

Marking numerically — according to achievement and the class norm — led to a massively repetitious process. Within a mark or two, the same children week after week scored eight, nine or ten on a ten-point scale; in like manner scores of three or four were accredited to another group of youngsters. This was honest appraisal of attainment — lapses could be heavily underlined in comments on exercise books, the blow of lowly achievement when children were clearly trying hard could be softened by encouraging words. Yet the whole procedure seemed phoney. My concern began with looking at a row of lowly scores recorded in my mark book opposite the name of a boy who had been striving his hardest to raise his standards. Latterly they had slid further back, yet I thought I had tried to give him every attention and encouragement. Was the lad beginning to unreservedly accept my judgement of him as declared so regularly in my marks? Was there here a mirroring of the self-fulfilling consequences we knew to exist in streaming? Children tend to live up (or down) to our expectations; they accept our appraisals of them and perform accordingly. When these evaluations are repeated regularly then frustration must surely result — particularly when the child is making every effort to improve. In a class wherein there are purposely placed children of widely differing abilities some must always excel according to the average attainments of the class, some will always be doomed to rank amongst the 'below average'. Had we removed the failure label from the class in which we placed many children only to pin it back on every time we saw their work?

Nothing succeeds like success. The adage may be hackneyed but its truth is evident with children. Somehow children have to be encouraged, their successes recognised as well as their inadequacies and failures. Children appreciate honesty, and we must not hide weaknesses where they exist, but in our marking schemes we must give credit where we can. This means being clear about our objectives. As in Mathematics teachers are concerned with a pupil's approach to a problem and pay attention to his working out of the solution at every stage rather than merely occupying himself with the final answer, so too we must be certain about what we seek from proffered pieces of work. The more I pondered over my problems of marking the more I realised that marking must be looked at in two dimensions — the evaluation of the attainment of knowledge, comprehension and skill elements I wished the children to gain and, secondly, the assessment of the sheer endeavour which had been displayed in striving after the attainment of these aims. Surely we could only expect children to give of their best? For this they merit credit, not continual adverse, interpersonal comparisons which can only have deleterious effects.

Several methods of recognition of both elements contained in the marking of work can be used. A personal answer was to record on pupils' work only an effort grade, marked on a five-point letter scale (A to E), with the uppermost point (A) indicating that from my point of view that child was doing his or her best. Of course this was subjective, of course it was meaningless in absolute terms, of course such grades were a shot in the dark in the early weeks of a session before I really knew children. Yet to children it was meaningful as a recognition of the effort they had produced in what was almost invariably an extended assignment task, taking several lessons and homeworks to complete. Linked to this grade was a fairly lengthy comment indicating the strengths and weaknesses of the piece, in terms of content, interpretation or style. The exercise — if it extended over three weeks — would already have been seen three times and brief annotations made, and so a final comment need not necessarily be lengthy as long as it was positive. In shorter, self-contained pieces — such as those in another language or, often, in Mathematics or Science — the same methods are possible and the points made ought to be reinforced and developed in class tutorial sessions.

Some of my present colleagues have argued quite reasonably that any mark or grade recorded is inevitably awarded a significance by pupils that it is not necessarily intended to convey. The accompanying comment tends then merely to merit a cursory glance. After all, letters and figures are readily comparable with those awarded to their friends! Thus, it is argued, the most important function of marking — to direct pupils, to encourage and help them towards improved standards — is being accorded a secondary rôle and its impact is less than it might be. Their answer is to write comments and to eschew any form of grading — at least in the children's books, though they record achievement and effort grades in their own mark books. Whilst this might not express a teacher's assessment as pointedly to children — especially to the less able — its virtues are evident in its highlighting of positive suggestions, to the exclusion of what might well be misunderstood detractions.

Others use a two-part system of marking, recording both

effort and attainment, which is defended on the grounds of
probity. Is it not honest, it is argued, to tell children exactly
where they stand, not only with regard to their own potential
but also with regard to all their classmates? Hence, two
parallel five-point recording systems are called into play. A to
E records attainment (it is based on five divisions in the class
or Year Group, either representing five sections, each
standing for twenty per cent of the class or year, or
approximating to a normal distribution curve of intelligence
with forty per cent scattered round the mean at C, ten per
cent at each extreme of the spectrum, A and E, and twenty
per cent in each of the other two segments) and 1 to 5
recording endeavour, or some similar variation of this
scheme. Thus C1 will indicate an exercise in which a pupil, in
the teacher's view, will have done his or her best and achieved
average attainment standards; A2 will place a child's work
amongst the best ten or twenty per cent of submitted
exercises, but reflect the teacher's opinion that that pupil
could have attained still higher standards with more effort.

Certainly this approach has the advantage of honesty,
certainly it has the advantage of simplicity as teachers
transfer the same mark into a record book giving them the
two measures they need for future reference. Yet, my
standard intuitive objection remains – to reinforce lowly
judgements at frequent intervals is to jeopardise chances of
improvement, and these intervals could be daily if a school's
whole teaching team is enjoined to adopt the same system,
which seems to me a less confusing procedure than the
individual methods so regularly used by teachers. Of course
the pill of failure is coated by high effort grades for those
pupils who are striving to raise their attainment levels, but is
this enough?

Whichever method is adopted to register achievement
levels in given pieces of work, the single, largely attainment-
based grade must be questioned in the context of mixed
ability classes. Though some teachers have always attempted
to absorb into this type of measuring unit a recognition of
endeavour on the grounds of humanity, in so doing they have
distorted scores and accordingly misled pupils and parents
alike. If grades are to be awarded for exercises undertaken,

they must surely all be within the reach of every member of a given class or teaching unit – and truly, not hypothetically, within their reach. The only exception to this might well be during an external examination course where teachers might wish to relate standards to those adopted by the examining board. To those who bring up the legend that children like to see marks on their books – a common enough comment in answer to my suggestion that ticking and re-marking on work might be sufficient – I would counter by questioning the validity of their assertion. Which children? High scorers or others? In what context? With or without comments? My annual anonymously completed questionnaires put to pupils in the first three secondary years as pieces of 'consumer research', seeking reaction to various topics and modes of working generally, suggested indifference to marks from the majority but that value was placed in remarks at the base of exercises. This was not the response I had anticipated, but I maintain that the results were not a function of the questionnaire method, though I accept that it might be pupil reaction to my own unconsciously expressed biases!

On the assumption that marking is not to admit of the termly or annual totting-up procedure to get aggregates of marks which allow inter-pupil comparisons to be made; that mark lists and Form positions are to be consigned to the educational refuse tip (together with Speech Days and the annual prize giving to a few pupils, generally the same children every year, whose genetic inheritances and constant supportive family backgrounds lead to success in only one aspect of school work), then Form and Year tutors, Heads of School and senior staff must be afforded some other means of being informed about pupil progress over a period of time.

Two systems commend themselves. If a school makes written reports to parents at termly intervals, involving comments on a series of subject areas, then half-termly reports which record effort – largely for internal use in the school – can be a simple matter. Nominal rolls of class members, together with a series of columns, allowing an insertion to be made in each subject, can be provided for staff. Pupils whose endeavours merit neither marked approval nor sterner comment need no inscription in the appropriate space, whilst slackers and those who are giving of their best can be recorded by the use of symbols such as minus and plus signs. This system, used at Settle High School, gave early-warning signs about deterioration in effort and allowed tutors to praise those whose efforts deserved it, though the files themselves remained confidential except that the information about both extremes of effort was passed on to the parents concerned (as will be discussed below).

At Radyr School written reports are sent to parents annually, in the summer term, whilst much importance is placed on the individual oral interviews to which each parent is invited in February or March. Much dissatisfaction has been expressed by parents and teachers when discussing parent interviews. The procedure whereby all teachers of a given Year Group are available at tables scattered in a large hall during one special evening leads to a bazaar-like atmosphere rather than one associated with the discussion of important matters. Teachers and parents are constrained by time pressures, by the queues behind them and by the lack of privacy. The length of queues and, often, the expected quality of the report (many parents only waited at the tables of teachers their children liked or did well with) conditions which subject teachers are consulted.

It was decided, therefore, to use a system of individual interviews between parents and Form Tutors in the Lower School where a largely common curriculum, based on mixed ability groupings, operates. Tutors during a given fortnight have the opportunity to use any two, three or more evenings, for however long they wish at a sitting, to meet individual parents, who normally choose a quarter-hour session from amongst those offered. Form Tutors have to have readily available a fund of information about children based on their academic progress as well as the social and interpersonal development about which they will have gathered inform-ation in personal contact, in informal discussions with Year Tutors and Head of School and in monthly tutorial meetings. To provide this information half-termly assessments of the progress of every child in every subject are prepared. These are confidential to staff but results can be passed on by Form Tutors (not subject teachers) to pupils or parents as seems necessary in individual cases. Such assessments record both attainment and effort on five-point scales as outlined above. They provide a tutor with a profile of a pupil's academic progress through a year, and three are available by the time of the oral interview. The Tutor will then discuss apparent declines and weaknesses with subject teachers and with pupils and use these records when interviewing parents who may, if they wish, be told of both grades given to their children, and have their meaning clearly explained.

Teaching mixed ability groups has led us to take an intense look at marking and assessing procedures. Whilst we retain an element of objective description of attainment levels, we have recognised other elements more clearly: the need to be aware of endeavour (for our ultimate goal must be to encourage all students to realise their own potentials); the need to encourage pupils; the need to highlight and to suggest remedies for deficiencies. Differential assessment standards in various subjects — roughly described by the indication that very high percentages were readily attainable in Mathematics whilst best performances in English, History or Religious Education gained numerically lower reward — have also been removed. Pupils and parents thus have a more valid picture of relative subject strengths and weaknesses. The essence of the whole procedure is, as in teaching, to see the child as an individual, to emphasise the importance of his or her achievements relative to his or her optimal performance as well as to that of others. The latter element, the crucial one, is deliberately fostered competitive situations in our schools, is put more truly into context in our efforts to stress that life and its manifold enterprises are about cooperation as well as competition, about the Boat Race and its joint efforts, as well as the Rat Race and the devil take the hindmost.

Pupil progress is, of course, to a large extent dependent on parental attitudes — interest or indifference, support or antagonism. Later the need to inform parents of developments and to help them to understand a system totally foreign to their experience will accordingly be discussed, for their rôle in furthering or retarding academic progress is a vital one. At this stage suffice it to say that, as in any other organisational system, the school must ensure the existence of an assessment system which parents can follow and so give support to the school in a meaningful way when this is found to be necessary – when a child is under-performing, for example.

Hence, at Radyr, the annual fortnight's session of interviews is only part of a reporting scheme, as are progress reports and interviews arranged whenever parents express concern about their children. The individual assessments made by staff at half-termly intervals are thus used not only for oral interviews. Parents of pupils who have achieved three top or three lowest effort grades (Grades One or Five) also receive written notification of this – an accolade or criticism which is thus open to all children, regardless of their ability level, every half-term. Though the most able do figure more largely in commendation lists, very many others receive similar encouragement.

At the end of each annual school session, written reports are again despatched to parents. The traditional pro formae were considered inappropriate, with their columns indicating position in class, termly attainment marks or grades, and short spaces for subject remarks within a column of such reports, leading to either abridged comments (what did 'average' mean, for example – every aspect of the pupil's performance in a given subject area?), or comments which were consciously or unconsciously conditioned by those preceding a teacher's own entry on the report. Our method of reporting gave up this approach and aimed for a single annual report which could be meaningful, detailed, honest and helpful. We adapted ideas we had seen elsewhere (at St Cyres School, Penarth, for instance) in order to try to bring these principles into play. Subject teachers were given pads of subject report slips, some six inches long and three inches wide, which were treated to allow duplicates of each slip to be made without the need for carbon paper. The only titles on these slips were Name, Form and Subject, and a box with spaces for Attainment and Effort Grades was set in one corner. Teachers at their leisure, during the last term of the year, complete these reports – one per pupil – and submit them to Form Tutors. These are then put in order, a general report written and despatched to parents in small card folders which explain the grading systems adopted. The duplicates are then stapled together and put into their place in the cumulative record file, which also contains marked spaces for the recording of half-term assessments.

The report sheet, it will be noted, contains no separate provision for examination marks. This is not to accept a corollary that testing and examinations are impossible in a mixed ability situation. Evaluation of progress — for teacher and taught — is necessary in every situation, but we must be fully aware of just what it is that we are measuring in any given instance. Too often in the past we have accepted that the end of term or end of session examinations that are traditionally part of the educational system measure all the skills and knowledge we wished a child to acquire as a consequence of schooling. The all-important atmosphere we created by our battery of examinations was often enhanced by a period of revision, the abandoning of the normal homework pattern and of the usual timetable itself, upheavals involving changes in the days' patterns of tuition and breaks and even the transfer and break up of form units to other classrooms or large spaces (to the PE specialists' disgust!) to minimise the dangers of copying. Did all this create a danger of distortion, of gross exaggeration of the significance of evaluation processes which can at best only test a few of the skills we see as important in schools? We lionise some skills — memory, performance under pressure, some developed attributes which lend themselves to testing in limited time conditions — and consequently, intentionally or otherwise, devalue others — research skills, use of initiative, patience, perseverance and industry, even cooperation, probity or determination. Thus examinations must be seen as part of a continual programme of assessment. Members of staff may cite these achievements or failures separately on report slips but it is not incumbent on them so to do. For the linguist laying emphasis on the oral achievements of their First Form pupils, the Handicraft teacher who can only sample work superficially in a limited period or the historian testing only a few of the cognitive areas with which he is concerned, these examinations cannot have the same importance as for the mathematician.

Where possible, then, examinations should be carried out with the minimum of upheaval — even within the framework of the normal timetable if possible. Block timetabling of a subject across a year group can of course make this possible, but in systems where different classes in a year group take like lessons at varying times then the formal examination perhaps becomes a necessity. Personally, I am convinced that the need for examinations ought to be decided at Departmental level — surely it is within the aegis of a subject Department to decide whether they will learn any more about skill achievement by their pupils from their performance under examination conditions? Are the skills of expression or creativity more accurately demonstrated to the English or Art teacher in the examination room than in the context of the normal class situation?

When the need for testing arises can it be done with groups of mixed ability? Is a test in such circumstances restricted by the spread of ability of the test subjects? Here the basic principles of the work sheet — entered into in some detail elsewhere in this book stand. As long as questions through the course of the question paper move along the twin axes of closed to open, and, even more important, from simple to complex, all candidates can be extended. One can in turn pose questions that demand simple recall and performance skills and then set tasks seeking more sophisticated attainment levels in areas of comprehension and application of recalled knowledge. Multiple choice questions providing three or four distractors to every key response are admirable vehicles for the testing of many subject areas — particularly as they can with greater validity test their declared objectives, without concurrently calling many other skills into operation, and at defined levels of difficulty. To these types of question can be added others which demand, successively, sentence, paragraph, or essay answers based on structures delineated — thus confronting candidates with more and more open-ended questions which provide opportunities for each to develop answers to greater or lesser depth.

The problem is little more difficult than that encountered in constructing any other form of examination based on the premise that the test must cumulatively assess achievement of certain declared objectives, and only those. If we have these objectives before us in any part of the syllabus then it is assumed that they have been deemed suitable to and attainable — if to varying degrees — by all students undertaking the course. Hence they must be examinable — if step by step, just as a teaching programme itself evolves. The only warnings to be advanced are the obvious — that the language must be comprehensible to all candidates and that all must have enough to do to occupy the whole of the test session. It is not sufficient merely to put in a few very simple tasks to encourage the less able initially then move to an elevated plane for a large proportion of questions. In Mathematics a succession of graduated questions — in terms of difficulty can be adopted, elsewhere situations can be contrived that admit of responses of varying complexity and detail. It is a mistake to believe that it is only complicated and difficult questions that bring about differentiation in responses. The English teacher who creates a picture of events in a few sentences and then asks for continuations or the geographer who describes a city site and hinterland and requests reasons explaining its growth will get qualitatively very diverse responses from these simple stems. In examining or testing, the same major criteria as in all other aspects of mixed ability work must be taken into account: can every individual cope with the initial demands of a question? Can everyone develop an answer which will enable him to demonstrate his real ability?

The essence of marking, assessing and reporting has traditionally been to find ways of ever more precise classification of children. At the institutional level youngsters have been classified according to the type of school they were allowed to attend — Grammar, Technical or Secondary Modern. Within these schools more and more precise categorisation has been sought in streaming and rank ordering in and across subject areas in their classes. Each child has been placed on the rungs of the ladder of achievement and been encouraged to prepare for the 'realities of life' by trying to clamber over fellow pupils to reach a higher step. Ultimately, only one can succeed; all the others are, in varying degrees, relative failures. If the crux of mixed ability work is concern with the individual, with the ability of each to ascend his or her own ladder of achievement to the top rung, then the systems of appraisal we adopt must reflect this. Any schemes of evaluation of progress must be positive, not fatalistic. Probity is necessary, but so, too, is encouragement. It seems trite to announce that credit must be given to pupils where possible, but how often has this been regarded in the highly competitive situations we structured? Education does not always trail in the wake of society; it can also fashion social emphases, priorities and patterns. If we are to say to our children that education — like life itself — is about doing one's best, pushing oneself to the limit in whatever one undertakes — cooperation as well as competition — then we must devise means of recording those elements and evaluating their achievement in our assessment procedures.

10 Conclusion

Any step in the dark must cause apprehension. Will one's leading foot come to rest on a solid base or, unexpectedly, in treacherous mud, or even, in an extreme, in the thin air of a chasm's mouth? In the traditional educational framework there are countless good teachers, teachers whose methods have evolved within the school pattern wherein they work. By judicious experiment and selection, by initiative and honest analysis of their teaching ploys, they have developed methods which in their limited fields of application work successfully. Yet, when their terms of reference and the organisational pattern which these underlie are found to be self-defeating, all must be subject to the closest scrutiny. This is not to say that everything must be rejected, merely to assert that if a new building collapses all parts of the construction process must be examined — plans, building methods and materials. If the framework is potentially dangerous, then, whatever skills are employed in building up the structure, it will always remain a hazard.

This is the problem of our traditionally streamed school pattern. If we accept the many inadequacies of streaming — and, in all honesty, can we do otherwise? — then we are morally obliged to de-stream our schools. This is the crucial decision — based on the rightness or otherwise of the system now in operation. We must not selfishly cling on to the past, to our proven methods in known situations and use these as a rationalisation for our denouncing of necessary change. It is indeed only human to feel insecure in the face of a totally unfamiliar work environment; equally, it is only natural that we should not wish to introduce a host of new problems when we feel that those we faced in our early days as teachers are now largely solved. To recognise that our past overall philosophy has been misguided takes considerable

courage; to then subject to scrutiny every practical corollary
of that philosophy demands even more moral strength. But it
must be done — the aim of this book has been to try to show
to practitioners that such readjustment is possible.

As with the first, much greater, step in the dark — the
adoption of comprehensive education — there have been
many voices deploring the loss of all that is best in British
education. The answer — to what is often cloudy nostalgia —
is that here is an attempt, not only to preserve what is best
but to make it available to all, and not merely to the élite
who have been chosen by the use of very dubious measures.
It has been my experience in unstreamed schools that there is
one regular, universal comment from visitors, indicating the
apparent happiness and involvement of children of all types.
Of course this is a generalisation and, as such, dangerous; of
course it could be the consequence of people seeing what
they want to see, yet it is what teachers have intuitively
recognised and regularly had confirmed. An atmosphere of
interest and involvement is surely the first prerequisite of
learning, and evidence is beginning to filter through that
organisation of schooling does make a difference. Dr
Thompson (1974), working in Coventry, has demonstrated
the effect that the abandoning of streaming has had on The
Woodlands. This school was rigidly streamed from its opening
in 1955 until 1961, after which it was banded until, in 1965,
mixed ability grouping was introduced to both Years 1 and 2
and extended to Year 3 in the following session. The
measures he used to evaluate the effects of change were the
numbers who remained at school, beyond the statutory
school-leaving age, to complete a full five-year course, and
performance at the Ordinary Level of the General Certificate
of Education. Thirty-seven per cent of the 1961 intake
stayed on, but this was more than doubled when he studied
the progress of boys who arrived at the school in 1967,
similar startling increases being recorded in other unstreamed
years (1965 — 64.4 per cent; 1966 — 70 per cent). Furthermore, this affected children of all abilities: inevitably the
greatest effect was apparent in boys of below average ability,
but there was a marked effect at all levels. There was, indeed,
a national tendency for pupils to remain longer at school in

this period; Coventry may have been more affected than most areas, due to frequent motor car industry recessions and lay-offs (though one could put the opposite view: that inflated wages in the car industry encouraged early leaving). Nevertheless, these figures from a single school are startling, whatever other variables were in operation.

To those who see the introduction of mixed ability groupings as a piece of social engineering which will only be achieved at the price of depressing academic standards, Dr Thompson's school provides sharp rebuttal. A quarter of the 1961 (the last) streamed intake achieved success in one 'O' Level subject; this was true of half of their 1965 (first, unstreamed) counterparts. The former registered 2.6 passes per pupil of the whole intake, the latter achieved significantly more with an average of 3.1 passes each. The percentage of students recording passes at every level increased — that is, in terms of gaining four, five or whatever clutch is studied — and, on average, even pass grades rose. One noteworthy feature of the report is that these improvements in performance were very evident in the achievements of the most able boys, who seemed now to have more chance of passing all subjects for which they were entered. This was especially noticeable with those who were entered for seven, eight or nine subjects. What price the 'lowered academic standards' theory? A single school experiment is not enough on which to build an argument, for hidden factors may well have been in operation. But, especially as measures were made over a series of years, there is certainly much food for thought here about the inter-relationship of non-streaming and improved academic standards.

Have we even seen here the greatest possibilities offered to us? Dr Thompson indicates that these achievements have been made in a school where 'basic techniques of class teaching' have been retained as the normative means of instruction. Much of what has been written in this book has been with the intent of encouraging teachers to devise methods which take into account the individual differences of our pupils. This is not pressing for the total abandoning of class teaching — on the contrary — but teachers are urged to create opportunities for pupils to achieve the best of which they are capable without our predetermination of these ceilings for them, according to some uncertain group norm.

These two factors are surely crucial to real education. Children must be helped to reveal and to fulfil their potentialities. We must maximise individuality or allow children so to do. It is as misguided to suggest that mixed ability groupings seek to disguise individual weaknesses in a somewhat dishonest fashion as it is to claim that standards of attainment will hover round those of the average pupils in a streamed class (whatever those may be). It has been truly said that what is wrong with Forms B,C,D, and E is Form A. Ascribed status that goes hand in hand with the streaming of pupils, teachers and facilities is counter-productive to any intention to allow youngsters to develop the abilities they have to the full and to develop personalities which have explored their own weaknesses and strengths as far as is possible. This is surely what streaming failed to do in tending to set generalised stream targets, which reduced the attainment levels of the more able in any group.

The placing of pupils in work groups which have prescribed ceilings and in which individual strengths and weaknesses are unrecognised (so that a 'B' child is supposed to achieve 'B' standards in all subject areas of the curriculum) must inevitably lead to feelings of resentment and rejection, especially, though not exclusively, by those who are seen as least able. The consequent non-cooperation, and even overt opposition, inside a school can defeat all our objectives. Mixed ability grouping is, then, not only an organisational pattern. This would be to dismiss it far too easily. It is part of an attitude which reflects a concern for each individual in the school community, a concern to avoid the rejection of any member of that community, a concern to allow each to show his or her worth — and not only in narrow academic terms.

Whilst the academic content of learning situations is important, other elements in the educational process must be fostered. It is not enough to allow pupils opportunities to grapple with the subject areas of our disciplines and hope that our other objectives will be attained in some magical fashion. We must structure the learning situation — inside and outside the classroom — in such a way that we will maximise the possibilities of their achievement. If we value tolerance, cooperation, initiative, individuality, honesty, the equal worth of all, or social awareness in the sense that all members of society should have some realisation of the problems faced by others, of their feelings, anxieties and attitudes, then we must plan for the attainment of these objectives in our schools. The adoption of mixed ability grouping is thus not merely a structural or organisational change: rather is it a total rethinking of our approach to formal education. This is perhaps why many schools which have rejected streaming have also rejected Speech Days or the publication of external examination results. Is it right that we should vaunt one aspect of our work at school whilst, in public terms, we ignore so many others — or find it impossible to formalise our praise? Is it right that some children — generally the same youngsters annually — should be publicly praised for doing their best whilst very many others are giving their all, often in a work situation which is much more foreign to them? Might not a three-subject 'O' Level pass which looks so insignificant at the side of an eight- or nine-subject clutch often really represent a much greater achievement by a student of relatively limited intelligence, whilst the more obviously successful candidate has taken things in his stride with little undue exertion? If we are to respect and give equal attention to all, this philosophy must infuse all our activities within schools. We must seek consciously to foster the strengths of each and try to help each to overcome weaknesses. Each child must be made to feel valuable and valued in our communities, and this attitude must be developed and planned for. For example, should the reception and guiding of important visitors to schools be the prerogative of the already socially acceptable able children? Youngsters working in a Remedial Department love the responsibility and need encouragement and opportunity in this way to help them overcome their often socially gauche manner. Similarly, why should Community Service projects be reserved for the least able, who are often all too aware of the problems of the more unfortunate members of the wider society outside school?

What is the cost of such a series of upheavals in a school? The biggest item in any survey of expenditure at the side of

gain in such a change is, putting it baldly, teacher wear and
tear. Within the classroom the mental agility and sheer
physical stamina demanded are great. Logically, if within
each class children are doing different things, with different
materials, at different levels then teacher adjustment must be
constant. At Secondary level, with changing classes at every
sound of the bell or buzzer, another set of adjustments has to
be begun and the process is repeated several times in the day.
Increased involvement by our pupils can often mean more
follow-up marking by teachers and more preparation to deal
with both anticipated and unforeseen demands. Yet these
pressures — faced for years by Primary School teachers,
especially in small schools where classes are often not
confined even to one chronological age group — are productive. How often in more traditional schools are vast
amounts of time and energy sapped in the pursuing of
problems, largely disciplinary, created by the large anti-
school group? How often are the seemingly successful and
enjoyable lessons with 'A' and 'B' Forms who never seem
demanding except in a pleasureable sense more than offset by
the wearying battles with Forms 'C' and 'D'? Of course the
truculent and ill motivated, the badly behaved and the
nuisance makers do not miraculously disappear with the
advent of non-streaming, but they are markedly reduced in
number as many of the reasons for their malbehaviour are
removed.

Side by side with these demands in our balance sheet must
come many professional advantages. Apart from the changes
consequent upon the more personalised relationships with
children, their generally improved attitudes, the opportunities for educational achievement in a wider sense than ever
before, it might, indeed ought to, be argued that teachers can
make gains which radically affect their own degree of
expertise. This is not to say that such changes can only be
achieved by setting up an unstreamed organisational pattern
but it is to assert that they should be consequent upon such a
change.

Anything which demands rigorous appraisal of what we are
doing is valuable. Of course we are continually involved in
such an evaluation of the methods we use daily, but how

often do we merely think at this relatively peripheral level without going back to why we are teaching a given topic or syllabus at all? Do we ask ourselves often enough about what we are really trying to do or do we just look at tomorrow or next week's lessons and ask ourselves questions about these? Perhaps one is too readily pessimistic or fatalistic in asking such questions, but in an ongoing situation it is not easy to stand outside the system to ask the really important questions. It is much more likely that we will become bogged down in the trivia of education. Many teachers have thus declared that, for the first time, they had to ponder, decide and articulate their objectives in both the operational terms of what they expect pupils to be able to do at given junctures in their school lives and in terms of priorities. In a subject area they had to ask themselves were they really trying to pass on only a body of factual information or a series of skills, irrespective of what the rest of the staff were seeking to do. How rarely have we discussed institutional aims couched in terms of 'What are we as a school trying to do with our pupils? What sort of end products do we want? How, as a school, can we achieve them?' Clarification of objectives must be the first prerequisite of improved modes of teaching.

Furthermore, the rejection of any established pattern should in the creation of a replacement lead to discussion, suggestion, counter suggestion, plan formulation and its acceptance or rejection amongst teachers within, and often across, Departments. This is not inevitable but probable, and the pooling of expertise, ideas and criticisms must be of benefit to practitioners, especially to those who are relatively inexperienced. Teachers are too often left in isolation the moment that they complete their probationary year, their autonomy respected, their problems their own. Departmental meetings do provide avenues for discussion additional to ad hoc staff room debate between individuals and groups, but these are generally about established practice and the ramifications thereof. Just as in team teaching or twin focus teaching, the use of the video tape-recorded lesson or the all-too-infrequent visit to someone else's lesson, here is an opportunity to gain cooperation at the basic level of teaching — in the planning of work, in the use of resources, in the discussion of approaches — at a time when such joint enterprise is made absolutely necessary by the facing of a massive and common problem.

One danger that should perhaps be indicated is that of over-hasty evaluation of any experiment on the grand scale. It is easy to over-react at a relatively early stage and to get things out of proportion. Teachers will not re-learn their trade overnight; it takes a considerable amount of time as well as courage to totally adapt — one is learning all the time. Especially must one remember that, concurrently, side by side with any limited experiment, there will be a contin- uation of traditional approaches, probably for the bulk of teachers' timetabled sessions. Further, if any experiment in mixed ability work is only allowed to proceed in a limited part of any group's timetable, it is difficult to establish how far practices in one subject area will undermine rather than complement those in another. In the one school there will be in juxtaposition at least two sets of totally dissonant objectives: success in the attainment of either can hardly be readily perceived. Additionally, children will take a long time to adapt. A factor which is often overstated is the resilience of children, their ability to shrug off change being frequently generalised from one or two examples. Children long used to being dictated to — literally and metaphorically — who associate education with little but rôte learning, teacher direction of pace and subject matter, imposed discipline and competitive situations, will not find the change easy. Reactions vary from comparisons to a holiday camp to pleas for more situations where 'teachers do the work'! The self-discipline, drive and self-direction associated with any more individualised programme is not easily developed.

Yet, the greatest step is the first. Much educational experience has suggested that what we want to achieve we can so do — given due diligence and perseverance. The first year of working in such a different situation can be harrowing; the work load will be heavy, doubts will always loom, but the pressure of work can be expected to be relaxed a little — as methods become more familiar, preparatory work from one session has carry-over to the next and pupils internalise the novel demands placed upon them. Must successful mixed ability grouping in the junior secondary years then be put to one side in the interests of meeting the demands of external examinations? Earlier, it has been suggested that this is not necessarily so — in some subject areas teachers have found it possible to deal with examination demands within a mixed ability context; others have introduced their own Mode Three G C E and C S E courses to ensure that examinations do not dictate what their students must do in their senior forms but, rather, assess what has been done. Others have rejected G C E Ordinary Level. With a single system of examining at 16+ now envisaged, and with the probable incorporation of Mode Three methods in that system, it is to be hoped that the possibilities now available will become more readily accessible and used.

At present we too often look for excuses to betray our principles; we know what we would do in the ideal situation but examinations, parents, resources and class sizes are used to delay decisions. This book has tried to reassure teachers that, despite their trepidation, the system wished for can work. Radyr staff were apprehensive and without experience in mixed ability work when the school opened in 1972. Doubts remain, but, in the middle of the 1973-4 session it was possible for some Fourth Form students — of all abilities — to be placed according to their subject choices in mixed ability classes for eighty-five per cent of their lessons. There was no separate R O S L A group; these children could each have been aiming at Ordinary Level or C S E certificates in some subjects. Mixed ability groups can work.

Bibliography

M. Asbell *Not Like Other Children* Redbook 1963

J.C. Barker-Lunn *Streaming in the Primary School* Newnes for the NFER 1970

C.W. Benn 'School style and staying on' *New Society* 24 June 1971

Board of Education (see also under Ministry of Education) *Handbook of Suggestions for Teachers* HMSO 1927
Report of the Committee of the Secondary School Examinations Council: Curriculum and Examinations in Secondary Schools (Norwood Report) HMSO 1943

W.R. Borg *Ability Grouping in the Public Schools: A Field Study* Dembar Educational Research Services 1966

A.B. Clegg 'Streaming in primary and secondary schools' *Forum* Vol. 5 No. 2 PSW (Educ.) Publications 1963

K. Coram 'An experiment in non-streaming in a new town junior school' *Forum* Vol. 4 No. 3 PSW (Educ.) Publications 1962

R.G. Crow *Teaching in Unstreamed Secondary Schools: Report of a Conference organised by the University of Exeter, Institute of Education* 1967

Crowther Report, Central Advisory Council for Education HMSO 1959

J.C. Daniels 'The effects of streaming in the primary school' Part II: 'What teachers believe' *Brit. J. Educ. Psychol.* Vol. XXXI 1961 (a) 'The effects of streaming in the primary school' Part II: 'A comparison of streamed and unstreamed schools' *Brit. J. Educ. Psychol.* Vol. XXXI 1961 (b)

R.P. Davies 'History teaching in an unstreamed comprehensive school' in *Teaching History* Vol. I No. 3 Historical Association 1970

J.W.B. Douglas *The Home and the School: A Study of Ability and Attainment in the Primary School* MacGibbon & Kee 1964

A.W. Foshay (ed.) *Educational Achievements of Thirteen-Year-Olds in Twelve Countries* UNESCO Institute for Education 1962

G.C. Freeland *Purpose and Method in the Unstreamed Junior School: New Trends in English Education* MacGibbon & Kee 1957

D.V. Glass *Introduction to the Home and the School: A Study of Ability and Attainment in the Primary School* MacGibbon & Kee 1964

M.L. Goldberg, A.H. Passow and J. Justman *The Effects of Ability Grouping* Teachers' College Press 1966

E.R. Guthrie *The Psychology of Human Conflict* Harper & Row 1938

D.H. Hargreaves *Social Relations in a Secondary School* Routledge & Kegan Paul 1967

B. Jackson *Streaming: an Education System in Miniature* Routledge & Kegan Paul 1964

C. Lacey 'Some sociological concomitants of academic streaming in a grammar school' *Brit. J. Sociol.* Vol. XVII 1966

Ministry of Education *The Nation's Schools* Pamphlet No. 1 HMSO, 1945 *Primary Education* HMSO 1959

National Foundation for Educational Research in England and Wales, *A Critical Appraisal of Comprehensive Education* Newnes 1972

Newsom Report *Half our Future* Central Advisory Council for Education HMSO 1963

G.V. Pape 'Accident of birth' *Education* 16 November 1956

D.A. Pigeon 'A comparative study of the dispersions of test scores' in *Educational Achievements of Thirteen-year-olds in Twelve Countries* (A.W. Foshay ed.) UNESCO Institute for Education 1962

R. Rosenthal and L. Jacobsen *Pygmalion in the Classroom: Teacher Expectation and Pupils' Intellectual Development* Holt, Rinehart & Winston 1968

C. Schiller 'Times are changing' *The Times Educational Supplement* 1 March 1963

B. Simon *The New Perspective: an Inaugural Lecture* Leicester University Press 1967

N.E. Svensson 'Ability grouping and scholastic achievement' (Report on a five-year follow-up study in Stockholm) *Stockholm Studies in Educational Psychology* No. 5 Almquist & Wiksell 1965

D. Thompson 'Towards an Unstreamed Comprehensive School' *Forum* Vol. 7 No. 3 PSW (Educ.) Publications 1965
'An experiment in unstreaming *Forum* Vol. 11 No. 2 PSW (Educ.) Publications 1969
'Non-streaming did make a difference' *Forum* Vol. 16 No. 2 PSW (Educ.) Publications 1974

P.E. Vernon *Secondary School Selection* Methuen 1957

D. Warwick 'Implications of Mixed Ability Group Work' New University and New Education 1969

G.E. Whalley 'Does transfer between streams work?' in 'Unstreaming in the comprehensive school' *Where* Supplement 12 Advisory Centre for Education 1968

C.J. Willig 'Social implications of streaming in the junior school' *Ed. Res.* Vol. V No. 2 1963

A. Yates (ed). *Grouping in Education* Wiley 1966

Notes on the authors

David Bosworth is at present lecturing in Education at Gwent College of Technology in Newport. He was formerly Head of Science at Kibworth, a Leicestershire High School.

R. Peter Davies taught History in a Coventry Boys' Comprehensive School before becoming Head of History at Settle High School, in the West Riding of Yorkshire. He is at present Deputy Headmaster at Radyr, a mixed Comprehensive School on the outskirts of Cardiff, and Head Designate of a similar school at Mynydd Isa in Clwyd — to be opened in 1978.

John Vickers has taught English to mixed ability groups at Settle High (Comprehensive) School in the West Riding, and in his present school, Minsthorpe Upper School and Community College, near Pontefract, where he is at present Head of the English Department.

Tony Warnes as Head of Modern Languages at Campion (Comprehensive) School, Bugbrooke, has taught French to mixed ability classes for seven years, during which time he has lectured widely on the subject and contributed articles to *Forum* and *At Classroom Level*.

Peter Wilcox taught Mathematics in a mixed Comprehensive School in Cardiff before becoming Head of Mathematics at Radyr.